G000167742

CONTEMPORARY APPROACHES OF THE SCIENTIFIC THEORY OF PLACE MARKETING - PLACE BRANDING IN GLOBALIZED CONDITIONS AND ECONOMIC CRISIS

BUSINESS ECONOMICS IN A RAPIDLY-CHANGING WORLD

Additional books in this series can be found on Nova's website
under the Series tab.

Additional e-books in this series can be found on Nova's website
under the e-book tab.

CONTEMPORARY APPROACHES OF THE SCIENTIFIC THEORY OF PLACE MARKETING - PLACE BRANDING IN GLOBALIZED CONDITIONS AND ECONOMIC CRISIS

ANDRONIKI KAVOURA, PH.D.

New York

Copyright © 2013 by Nova Science Publishers, Inc.

For permission to use material from this book please contact us:
Telephone 631-231-7269; Fax 631-231-8175
Web Site: http://www.novapublishers.com

NOTICE TO THE READER

The Publisher has taken reasonable care in the preparation of this book, but makes no expressed or implied warranty of any kind and assumes no responsibility for any errors or omissions. No liability is assumed for incidental or consequential damages in connection with or arising out of information contained in this book. The Publisher shall not be liable for any special, consequential, or exemplary damages resulting, in whole or in part, from the readers' use of, or reliance upon, this material. Any parts of this book based on government reports are so indicated and copyright is claimed for those parts to the extent applicable to compilations of such works.

Independent verification should be sought for any data, advice or recommendations contained in this book. In addition, no responsibility is assumed by the publisher for any injury and/or damage to persons or property arising from any methods, products, instructions, ideas or otherwise contained in this publication.

This publication is designed to provide accurate and authoritative information with regard to the subject matter covered herein. It is sold with the clear understanding that the Publisher is not engaged in rendering legal or any other professional services. If legal or any other expert assistance is required, the services of a competent person should be sought. FROM A DECLARATION OF PARTICIPANTS JOINTLY ADOPTED BY A COMMITTEE OF THE AMERICAN BAR ASSOCIATION AND A COMMITTEE OF PUBLISHERS.

Additional color graphics may be available in the e-book version of this book.

Library of Congress Cataloging-in-Publication Data

ISBN: 978-1-62948-202-6

Published by Nova Science Publishers, Inc. † New York

This book is dedicated to Stavros, who believes in me
Kelly, who is always there
George, Ourania, Evi, who helped me to move on

CONTENTS

PREFACE

Contemporary economic crisis is one of the biggest ones in global economy and has been forcefully applied to the real economy, revolting in a deep recession. Globalization has in turn contributed to the faster transmission of the problem from country to country.

This crisis disproportionally affects countries with small and medium development but also the medium and low social layers and small and medium entrepreneurship within countries. The stability of employment has fallen apart. The consequences of the economic crisis have brought out systemic problems and distortions in different sectors of productive activity; local communities and prefectures are examples of places in which, experience these consequences. The power of brands of significant value and businesses at the global level, have also collapsed.

The economic crisis also creates huge problems to the tourism sector which mainly consists of small and medium enterprises in southern European countries. This resulted in the tourist agents becoming unable to accommodate their customers' needs.

Traditional marketing as it is known is insufficient not only to the merchandizing product sector but also to the services sector, with the marketing of place branding to face the most serious problems.

To this cross-road, the societies, the places, in total, are called to find ways to exit from the crisis, to think positively and to motivate all their resources and their productive forces, employing all the local resources of the natural and human environment.

We should not though, identify the brand and the marketing of a place - that are associated with a multiplicity of relations in places- with the techniques of marketing that are adopted in the business sector and that is why the term advertising has not been used for places, cities, countries; Anholt

(2010) specifies that the techniques of competitive identification and marketing may be useful when a product or a service is sold, that is why, advertising campaigns in tourism are effective; countries and places are 'not for sale', that is why, in the branding strategy of a place, city planners should keep in mind that we talk about a transfer of successful corporate procedures of the private sector, to the public sector of the city or the place.

Within this horizon, place marketing is called to play a significant role for societies' revival and their exit from the crisis, but also for the reassurance of social cohesion and motivation of all the local forces in such a way so that the demanded synergy is accomplished. The main tools of this new model of place marketing are the internet and the networks. This is one of the most important innovations of this research.

In addition, it relates, as a main basis and point of departure, the identity of a place with its brand and e-brand, in order to safeguard its public interest and the necessary participation and motivation on the part of the community thus, enhancing social cohesion. Furthermore, it directly relates the visitors with the region and the 'imagined community' which may reinforce the brand and its position to the preferences of the group.

Finally, it introduces a new methodology for the design of communication strategies and a marketing and branding model for the places in the areas of Europe, without this necessarily to mean that they cannot be applied to other regions in the world with common characteristics.

Its scientific innovation relies in the systemic approach for place marketing and place marketing design. It is the first time that the relation of the imagined community, the public interest and social cohesion are attempted to be connected with the entrepreneurship and directly related with the free market of the scientific management theory. This emerges as the unique tool for exit from the crisis for all the rural and urban or semi-urban places while at the same time, it reinforces and stabilizes the identity of this place. To this direction, it employs all new technologies to the maximum degree. Finally, it proposes a new holistic model of place marketing based on the theory of networks with the use of internet incorporating terms and methods of political science and social policy for a sustainable and human development of the regions. This is an ongoing research in order to deepen the interplay between networks and place identities but also to develop the methodology from the feedback and information that will emerge from the implementation of this model in real life. In particular, our research for place marketing had a focus on the Rural Tour CADSES project and continues with other places aiming through the specific methodology which was developed within the programme and the other case studies not incorporated in the programme to examine the validity and reliability of the methodology and strategic design of place marketing, place branding but also to create a unified model/ proposal for different areas with common characteristics.

In contemporary conditions, place identity has a significant role to play, is in the first line and is reinforced from national identity. The strategic plans for the promotion of a place are based on national and place identity implemented from key players. The key players to a marketing plan for the promotion of a place and its branding are the private sector, the public sector, the human resources -internal and external-, the implementation of new technologies, the media and the internet as communication tools, the natural capital of each place, the social capital of the place and its cultural capital. This results into a place branding that is chosen by people. The connecting element of the successful place branding and place marketing can be the social public interest.

This monograph consists of a useful tool for academics, researchers, educators, tourism policy makers, advertisers, marketers and students but also for the local communities of various regions in order to be able to design a real exit from the crisis.

Chapter 1

PLACES AND REGIONS IN THE HORIZON OF GLOBALIZATION AND ECONOMIC CRISIS

INTRODUCTION

Contemporary economic crisis is one of the biggest ones in global economy and has been forcefully applied to the real economy, having as a result a deep recession and employment reduction. Globalization has in turn contributed to the faster transmission of the problem from country to country. In the last years, the global community experiences many changes to all political, economic and social sectors and each population makes titanic efforts to preserve their national identity but also the quality of their everyday life high. Thus, countries in the globalised world opt to promote their distinct characteristics and retain a position in the global world opting for the presentation of a unique identity.

Political situations, environmental factors, the international political environment, economic and social factors are significant and determine the policies which will be designed and implemented for the promotion of a region, a state, a city. Economic, political, social and sociopsychological parameters may contribute to the presentation of identity of a place since places need to differentiate themselves from each other to assert their unique and distinctive characteristics (Pritchard and Morgan, 2001; Kavaratzis and Ashworth, 2008; Kuscer, 2013; Katsoni, 2011). The continuous interstate circulation of information and products is also accompanied from the movement of populations, cultural characteristics and economic transactions. This trend of central control and attempt to homogenize of the distinct characteristics of populations is called globalization and is perceived as positive by some people and negative by others, based on their political beliefs or social status; on the other hand, the interdependent world we live, suggests that the concept of localization continues to give power to the nation state which remains important with its powers of action redefined rather than the argument that globalization heralds the end of the power of the nation state (El Sayed and Westrup, 2003: 79). There is free movement of goods among countries with Europe but also all over the world, thus, exclusive territorial rights cannot be used to prevent the importation of specific products, not to mention the general mobility that exists among products and people (Kavoura, 2006: 182).

Therefore, such central control is inevitably met in the three fields of social life:

- economy and rules of regulation of production, of exchange, of distribution and of products' and services' consumption
- policy and the terms of concentration and exercise of power and jurisdiction, diplomacy and the surveillnance of media and coercion
- culture, transmission of messages, beliefs, preferences and values but also the production and use of symbols (Thompson, 1995).

Based on the above mentioned, globalization, may be analyzed in seven types according to Petrella (1996):

1. Globalization of financial markets and the possession of capital
2. Market globalization and strategies of competition
3. Globalization of technology, knowledge and research
4. Globalization of ways of life, consumer behaviors and culture
5. Globalization which leads to the change of role of national governments and leads to the global governance
6. Globalization as a political unification of the world
7. Globalization of a person's perception and feeling for the world which leads to the establishment of 'one land' and of 'the global citizen' (Petrella, 1996).

Therefore, in our age, the capital but also employment is 'globalized'. More specifically, in regard to the capital, as a starting point, we could set the emergence of capitalism during the 15th century. The theory of capitalist economy, as it was argued by Adam Smith in the 18th century is exactly based on the hypothesis of full mobility, globalization and internationality of productive factors (Souder, 2010). Regarding employment, a simple reading of history is enough to illustrate that the migration flows and employees' movement had exceeded every limit during the 19th century (needless to refer to the slavery period for example which laid the African Continent in ruins since the 16th century) -so that nowadays movement to be comparatively presented as insignificant.

Having 'globalization' as an excuse, nowadays populations encounter a catalysis of the social capital and not only the state's freedom and independence is aimedto be limited -even in Europe which gave birth to it as a concept, and to which, has long before indisputably offered proof of economic success and performace (Alonso and Bea, 2012).

Therefore, under the mask of globalization nowadays, there is the granted will of governments and the political personnel to quickly globalize economy, to the advantage of an extremely small minority, which will prevail, irrespective of how counter productively this operates, even in capitalist terms.

The result of all the above mentioned, is that in the last years, global community experiences an economic crisis of big depth, which, even if it was originally manifested in the USA -having been associated with bank debts and more specifically, the inability of paying the mortgage loans-, it soon became epidemic.

Economic crisis expanded rapidly in the developed countries and following to the whole world, with dramatic consequences to the bank system and businesses. According to the International Monetary Fund, the crisis has been forcefully transmitted to the real economy, having as a result recession and decrease of employment which Europe experiences nowadays (Global Financial Stability Report, 2011).

Within this horizon, global economic news reports offers us a specific definition of the concept of crisis, focusing on the bank and economic system of countries. Nevertheless, this term incorporates many other concepts, such as cultural crisis, value crisis etc. Initially, this term meant the decision to solve a problem so that a country, a business, an organisation etc could come out from a difficult situation. The crisis is an unusual situation which is characterized from instability and places and regions are the first to be influenced from the consequences of the international speculators.

Many examples can be mentioned, the most typical of which is the one from the countries of South Europe but also of Island and of specific regions of Americ. We observe that the examples are not missing in order to show that the regions, the places, the countries, the prefectures, the communities, are mainly the ones to experience the crisis. Nevertheless, beyond economic crisis, the place encounters many different types of crisis. A territory is in crisis because of its confrontation with a difficult and unexpected situation which cannot deal with. This situation which holds in time unavoidably influences the economy, but also the social relations, the identity and the image of the place.

Contemporary crisis, directly related with the globalization conditions inflicts the central core of societies, the one which consists of the place identity and people's identity.

THE FACTORS LEADING TO CRISIS

The crisis is sudden but not abrupt. It is often the result of bad management of economic, social or political governance aspects. In the case of contemporary crisis, its presence is due to an instable way of governance which is based on assumptions about a non sustainable economic model (Alonso and Bea, 2012). For the regions, which adopt this non sustainable business model on a long term basis, this limits the possibilities of development of local agencies, confining in that way, the capital investment and thus, the sources of income for the community. Nevertheless, the crisis is not only associated with the problem of the economic management. Within the framework of globalization and free market nowadays, communities are faced with the increase of competition between regions, regarding the maintenance and attraction of investors; in the framework of tourism, the attraction of tourists is the point of interest (Papp and Raffay, 2011). For this aim, the community should be very competitive in regard to the facilities offered (business tax, financing etc); businesses aim to the profit. Nevertheless, when a community cannot or does not anymore offer the benefits to the market activities and to the capital, businesses leave the country, the periphery, the place in search of more profitable opportunities. This phenomenon leads to what may be described as industrial crisis (Global Financial Stability Report, 2011).

The socio-political factor is also a significant trigger for a crisis. Every region, irrespective of its abilities, aims to the social cohesion, the development of motives. Public policies have a significant role to play in order to mainatin social cohesion. They mainly need to safeguard equality and solidarity between citizens in a democratic system. Nevertheless, when the public realizes that these democratic principles are not kept, then, the crisis is inevitable.

There are also many other reasons of crisis: those associated with socio-demographic factors (for example, youth migration and specialized workforce), with historic ones (for example, the consequences of a war), political-institutional (for example, lack of identification of the regions and their mechanism with the countries). Destabilization of one or more identity elements of identification with the region, tangible or intangible -since a region may have tangible and intangible elements (Mitsche et al., 2013)-, distorts the real place identity but also its formation as well, leading in that way, to its destabilization. To all the abovementioned consequences, we highlight one important common element, crisis has consequences to the region's economy.

CRISIS' CONSEQUENCES AND THE CHANGES IT BRINGS

Apart from the disruption of economic stability, within the regions, the crisis negatively influences the public and elected officials but also the private sector such as businesses; the crisis consists the source not only of the economic decline but also of the identity decline because of the creation of negative images for the region which is damaged from crisis and economic recession. Cases from industrial municipalities suffer the most from econommic crisis as is the case in the Swedish Bergslagen region; research illustrated that in peripheral and economically vulnerable regions across Europe with experiences of negative economic development and unfavourbale imaages, there is need to implement marketing strategies to attract tourists, business but also inhabitants of the region in an attempt to boost the identity and the distinct elements of the region (Cassel, 2008).

Therefore, it is clear that crisis has an impact on the identity. Whether they are socio-economic, socio-political, socio-demographic crisis, they expand to all layers of the population of an area, they create phenomena of exclusion of poverty and decline, crisis is many times the reason of violent social conflicts. Thus, the system of representations of human beings is disrupted. Humans need to feel accepted and be recognized by other people, which is an issue of respect and trust. Material heritage contributes to provide prestige and dignity for a population; "The material cultural heritage is particularly suited to helping to develop the population's awareness of a shared historical identity" (Herrmann, 1989: 35). Archaeological heritage sites constitute a resource mobilized to provide a material link between the past and the present and serve to anchor collective memory for a given population conferring prestige and dignity (Smith, 1984: 102; Kristiansen, 1989; Van den Abeele, 1990). The demolition of cultural heritage and its symbolic elements may cause loss of the symbols of recognition of the region/place or on the contrary, contribute to provide an alternative way of presenting a place's myths of nationhood through architectural buildings for example (Palonen, 2013). Religion in Lalibela, Ethiopia, is at the forefront of the society's cohesion; the totem poles of Ninstints act as a focus for the resurgence of interest in ancient culture; and the Polynesian culture on Rapa Nui acts as the reinfocement of identity (Carlisle, 1998; Shackley, 1998).

As Palonen (2013) argues, the choice of elements which allow people to differentiate from others is of vital significance for the procedure of the creation of identity as was the case in the definition of the Hungarian national identity. As a result, territorial crisis leads to the loss of trust and the points of reference and thus, to the loss of place identity. Humans do not anymore feel that they belong to the latter having the sense of missing space, do not anymore recognize the points of reference with which they cannot identify anymore and for which they used to have more respect (Palonen, 2013).

If crisis has the power to inflict a real loss of place identity, this takes place because with its prevalence, it has first and for most dramatically damaged its image. Identity consists of an integral part of the image (Bellou, 2013; Ren and Ooi, 2013). As Ren and Ooi (2013) argue, national identity is asserted via the process of communicating identity to oneself, this is called auto-commuication and organizes a sender around its own perspectives and images. But what happens in the emergence of crisis? businesses may move to cheaper locations or there is migration of young people but also the migration of specialized human resource, facts which may lead to the reduction of the attractiveness of these places, especially if the communities do not have the means to maintain their competitiveness, in order to remain attractive (Alonso and Bea, 2012). Therefore, if crisis plays a significant role for the attractiveness of a place and the reduction of its competitiveness, one may assume that crisis has a significant impact on the territories' images, based on the fact that it influences its fame. Place branding may improve the development of a region or country and is becoming a powerful tool to gain competitive advantage; in that way, it may attract investment, new residents, jobs and skilled migrants but also tourism (Alonso and Bea, 2012).

The region, the place exists only if it has an identity, which derives from and is constructed from the people who live or have lived or wish to live there

(Mitsche et al., 2013). Identity may convey a specific image, that of the image of the territory /place of a region. The place/ territory of a region, which in turn, due to the human but also the natural environment are interconnected and are dynamic elements, has an impact on identity. It is a cycle that can be virtuous or vicious in the case of peripheral crisis. Peripehries and regions which are faced with the loss of the sense of self and the recognition from other people -as we have mentioned above (see Herrmann, 1989: 35; Palonen, 2013)-, are quickly led to a loss of attractiveness and loss of their fame.

With the arrival of globalization, the identity of a country, a place, a region becomes blurred and contries, places, regions need to promote, communicate and market their distinct elements to the competitive world to different audiences (Ren and Ooi, 2013). As a result, and under the conditions previously described, the discussion whether place marketing can be a solution for the reversal of this situation, emerges as an issue of high importance and emergency.

Chapter 2

MARKETING AND PLACE MARKETING AT THE FOREFRONT OF NEW CONDITIONS OF ECONOMIC RECESSION AND CRISIS IN SEARCH FOR A NEW ROLE

MARKETING NOWADAYS

Marketing is defined as the procedure of determining the needs and the wishes of consumers. Thus, the business or the organization should be in a position to offer products that satisfy the needs and the wishes of their consumers-customers (Whalley, 2010: 11).

Marketing incorporates all the necessary activities in order for a product to be distributed from the producer to the consumer. Marketing begins with the market research, continues with the procedure in which traders need to know as much as possible for consumers' needs and wishes and ends when someone buys the product. For businesses, the production, advertising, transportation, processing, packaging and sales are included in the marketing process (Whalley, 2010).

In order for the marketing process to operate, in other words, in order for consumers to have the opportunity to buy the products and the services which are necessary, nine important operations should be completed. These operations are the following:

- Market: humans have the opportunity to buy the products they want
- Sales: operation of producers in a free market in order to sell their products to the consumers
- Financing: banks and other financing organizations offer money for production and trading of products
- Storage: products need to be stored and be protected till the time the consumer needs them. This operation is highly significant for sensitive products (Ampuero and Vila, 2006).
- Transportations: Products should be transferred to the areas where consumers may buy them. This is a very important function. In transportations, rail, sea, air, overland are included and telecommunications for non tangible products, in other words, for services
- Processing: Processing is the procedure where raw materials go through a process in order to be able to be used from the consumer
- Risk taking: Insurance companies provide coverage for the protection of producers and traders from loss which is due to fire, stealing or natural disasters
- Market information: Information from all over the world in relation to the market conditions, weather conditions, price fluctuations and every change which may influence the trade procedure. Information about the market provided from all forms of telecommunications such as television, internet and telephone and other communication and advertising media are also included (Belch and Belch, 2009)
- Selection and standardization: Many products are rated so that they comply with the quality standards that have been determined. In that way, the product quality is guaranteed but also the consumer's safety (Zotos, 2008; Whalley, 2010: 44; Belch and Belch, 2009).

In that way, we may argue that the concept of holistic marketing proposed by Kotler and Keller (2012) and was incorporated in their book marketing management incorporates the abovementioned elements. The theory of marketing consists part of the integrated marketing communications concept which is employed as the basis for the internal idea of marketing and as a solution of dealing with the economic crisis from businesses (Belch and Belch, 2009). Holistic marketing incorporates internal market, safeguarding that all in the business or an organization adopt and follow the appropriate principles of marketing, especially those members who are high in the hierarchy (Kotler and Keller, 2012; Koutouzis, 1999).

Internal market is in charge of hiring personnel, educate and provide them with motives in order to better serve the business's customers (Koutouzis,

1999). Visionary businessmen recognize that marketing activities within the company, may be significant to the same degree or even more significant from marketing activities applied outside the business. There is no point to promise excellent service, when the company's personnel is not ready to provide such services (Kotler et al., 2001). Employees should be considered as customers and they are significant for the company since they are the at the forefront of communication with the customers; thus, all activities should be cooperated and enorchistrated based on consumers' point of view where the members high in the hierarchy take the decisions taking into consideration all the related departments in order to reach a feasible, appropriate and approved strategy (Vinieratou et al., 2003: 54-55; Kotler et al, 2001). Therefore, a network of cooperation and coordination of activities is essential which will allow people -employees, stakeholders, consumers- to promote the idea of the product or service, which is in our case the place or region.

Nevertheless, crisis nowadays is a crisis which disputes traditional functions of all postindustrialist era. A crisis that reaches the core of the human contract, questioning concepts that were the foundations for 100 years; this is trus if we consider that work stability has fallen apart; the promise of a pension in compensation to payments made by the employee in his/her job or to the traditional self-employment has also fallen apart while umemployment has increased (Izzo, 2012). The power of brands equivalent to global logos and businesses of significant value has also collapsed. The system of traditional maketing which did not incorporate the customer to the procedure of production and distribution, inserting multiple levels of intermediaries and allocated advertising cost, promotion, distribution to the final product price, not only does it collapse but also from these levels of intermediaries and employees, the biggest unemployment is created. The consumer has such an important role who is also incorporated in the product innovation process employing qualitative research methodologies to understand their perspective (Sakellariou and Karantinou, 2013).

Nowadays, two axes will characterize the new trade organization; internet marketing and network-clusters marketing. The solutions which will both combine will be more powerful. Many companies associated with traditional trade -if they have not developed them yet-, they develop internet marketing as an alternative distribution channel to elevate and rejuvenate their company.

CAN MARKETING APPLY TO REGIONS AND PLACES IN GENERAL

A. The Complexity of the Definition

Can the concept of marketing apply to places or territories especially in a period of economic crisis where companies redefine their aims and take into consideration the consumers and the role they have to play in all states of marketing? Marketing is no longer to be associated with business firms; marketing of nations where the marketing of place is also incorporated can be the case (Skinner and Kubacki, 2007: 305).

A place may promote its image for attracting tourists by providing a competitive advantage. Therefore, regions promote themselves and their perceived competitive advantage (Kavoura, 2005; Kavoura, 2007; Hall and McArthur, 1993; Pritchard and Morgan, 2001). It is then, that elements of marketing management are adopted by the promotion of places (Bitsani and Kavoura, 2010). According to Kotler, Haider and Rein (1993) the S.W.O.T. analysis of the marketing factors (infrastructure, attractions, image and quality of life and people) where S stands for strenghts, W for weaknesses, O for opportunities and T for threats may be well applied for the marketing of places.

Three concepts need to be defined, in order to provide a definition of marketing which can be valid at the territorial level. First, the concept of the market; the market can be the typical or virtual place of the merchandized products or services of various goods. It also represents in the broad sense everything included in a place/ territory, consumers, or/and possibilities that a product or a service has. Thus, the concept of territorial 'purchase' seems difficult to be defined and be evaluated, it is difficult to determine its outline within specific boundaries. The tourism destination as a place is hard to outline and that is why whole countries are chosen as tourist destinations not for being competitive, which is is not the subject matter anymore but to increase tourism expenditure, to increasingly attract visitors, to satisfy and provide them with memorable experiences; at the same time, residents are happy and the natural capital of the destination is preserved (Ritchie and Crough in Papp and Raffay, 2011: 23). Can the territorial 'market' be identified with the administrative bourdaries of this place/ territory, recognizing the subjectivity and multiplicity of the beliefs of this living place; Within this framework, we define the territorial aspect (or territororial place) of the market as follows: it is the administrative place within which but also around this place all the products and services are incorporated and the direct 'consumers' may enjoy because of that proximity.

Second, there is the concept of the customer or the consumer. The customer is a legal entity or a person to whom we aim to sell a product or a service. In regard to a territory or a place, we may have our final customer, the visitors, the residents of a place but also businesses, internal and external associations; these are the stakeholders of the place and may contribute to its place marketing. Stakeholders may be residents who can be also managers in the region, they want their businesses to be successful and viable and their primary work is often associated with tourism (Bitsani and Kavoura, 2014- who examined the attitudes of the community of Istria, Croatia towards the promotion of rural and cultural tourism of the area). Residents may become committed to the region's branding and advertising efforts and actively participate to the region's promotion, including themselves to such a branding procedure and presenting themselves as being part of the identity of the region (Kemp, Williams and Mordelon, 2012; Kerrigan, Shivanandan and Hede, 2012; Kuscer, 2013; Sartori, Mottironi and Antonioli, 2012); they feel a strong connection for the promotion of the destination since they actually promote themselves, their businesses, their values, their traditions, their home. Destination stakeholders include public sector and governments, residents, tourism industry sector, destination management organization and other groups-such as the most important categories which may influence and determine the management and marketing Goeldner and Ritchie in Konečnik, 2004). The effort needs to be made not only to outsiders such as tourists, but rather to residents themselves, the inhabitants of the place, who need to see the attractiveness of the region in order to be able to market it in a sustainable way (Cassel, 2008; Braun, Kavaratzis and Zenker, 2010).

We should not though, identify the brand and the marketing of a place - that are associated with a multiplicity of relations in places- with the techniques of marketing that are adopted in the business sector and that is why the term advertising has not been used for places, cities, countries; Anholt (2010) specifies that the techniques of competitive identification and marketing may be useful when a product or a service is sold, that is why, advertising campaigns in tourism are effective; countries and places are 'not for sale', that is why, in the branding strategy of a place, city planners should keep in mind that we talk about a transfer of successful corporate procedures of the private sector, to the public sector of the city or the place.

The fact that residents and stakeholders in a place can be consumers of the place but they may also simultaneously be or become partners and agents of this place as has been described above, may complicate the academics' and professionals' work of place marketing. As a result, we cannot talk about a customer, but in general about the broad term of participation, that is, the concept of customer in place marketing is associated with all those who, inside or outside this place participate in any way as active subjects to the life and development of the place. Thus, policy makers in charge of place marketing and marketers who initiate communication and advertising strategies and campaigns need to take into consideration that the inhabitants of a place are a significant target market that they need to approach and attract (Cassel, 2008). This then, can be a developmental tool especially in peripheral and economically vulnerable regions across Europe where residents may realize the significance of cultural economic approaches to development (Cassel, 2008; Kemp, Childers and Williams, 2012). Povilanskas and Armaitiene (2010) argue that the key to tourism competitiveness for a region, a country, a place is the power actor-networks have for marketing the region.

Last, the concept of the offer in a market in the sense of trade businesses, which is associated with the production of products. In the case of place marketing, different associations which operate in the place of communities, develop and manage the place through urban and environmental projects, public infrastructure, cultural and athletic blocks, sites and others, residencies and business places, stations etc which improve the place and provide it with life and essence. What is on offer to be promoted in a place may be physical and material aspects but also intangible qualities (Mitsche et al., 2013: 69).

B. Place Marketing-Conceptual Definitions

A specific definition for place marketing among academics and practitioners does not exist and yet this concept does not have universal acceptance; nevertheless, there are common concepts (Kavaratzis and Ashworth, 2008; Skinner and Kubacki, 2007) and these are associated with attractiveness, competition and development. These are elements which illustrate that places are nowadays facing new problems of competition which demand to develop their image, in order to attract highly status investors and personalities of international fame.

Thus, we may define place marketing as a procedure which aims to the elevation of what the place offers, in the sense that this becomes more attractive. Place marketing should provide solutions to the needs of the participating parts. For example, the community works on a plan and develops it for the restoration of an abandoned place. Its aim is to transform it to a truly living place which will be characterized from commercial activities and cultural events. As a result, it needs to construct buildings to which a specific meaning should be attached. This is exactly where the role of place marketing lies: to define this place as an area of culture and trade. In that way, it may be improved and be elevated with quality terms, giving in that way, real life and meaning to it. Then, place marketing will aim to attract the external audience or the external environment with its cultural, tourist and economic sustainability in order for this audience to come as investors or visitors. The tangible and intangible elements of a place, a destination and its heritage may act as the magnet for others to see, invest, work (Mitsche et al., 2013: 69).

It is thus significant to appeal to these people in order to make them participants in all the phases of tourism development of a place. When residents trust and are committed to a place, they may form such strong connections with it that it becomes reflective of their self-concept (Kemp, Childers and Williams, 2012). Limited research on the significant role of the communication with stakeholders in the planning process but also in the implementation stage though exists although collaboration and cooperation among stakeholders in order to bring about common good for the community and enhance their own interests is an issue that should be sought (Karvelyte and Chiu, 2011; Ooi and Pedersen, 2010; Northover, 2010; Bitsani and Kavoura, 2014).

Place Marketing and Tourism- Being in Parallel Lives

Nowadays, it is typical that standardized and mass tourist packages do not cater for tourists' needs. People realized the problems that could be created by the prevalent model of mass tourism and they were driven to search for alternative forms of tourism (ecotourism, rural tourism, cultural tourism, historic tourism). These forms respect the local community and its visitors but also the cultural heritage and the environment (http://www.conservation.org/xp/CIWEB/programs/ecotourism/ecotourism.xml; Bitsani and Kavoura, 2010: 307). In that way, a place promotes its image for attracting tourists by providing a competitive advantage by "using business and marketing strategies that aim at adapting to the changing conditions, offering the required value to potential customers and sustaining its development and vitality" (Papapetropoulos and Zondiros in Bitsani and Kavoura, 2010: 307).

Based on the resources available, the unique selling proposition is created for the selected attractions of the place -with the promotion of physical and soft or immaterial attraction factors (Kotler et al. in Rainisto, 2003: 70; Mitsche et al., 2013). In that way, the sum of characteristics that differentiate the place from other places are necessary, offering a way of life, communicating it to target groups to show its advantage (Rainisto, 2003: 74-75). It is then, that elements of marketing management are adopted by the promotion of places.

Bitsani and Kavoura (2013) argue that the success of tourism does not only depend on specific tourist services (hospitality, transport, dining, etc) but also on general factors which influence the experience tourists gain such as: advertising of the promotional material before visiting the area, reservations, the trip to the area, the first welcome, information about the area, accommodation and dining infrastructure, the sights to be visited, hospitality, issues of hygiene and safety, the natural environment, the farewell, the return journey but also the possibility of getting in touch and communicating with the community keeping the memories alive (European Commission, 1999; European Committee, 2000; Bitsani, 2004; Bitsani and Kavoura, 2010). The results for the reduction of the peripheral inequalities are positive in general, although they differ from country to country since a basic factor for the proper use of the economic resources of each country is the structure of the economy of each country.

Traditionally, people with different backgrounds and professional orientation are associated with cultural tourism, such as officers of museums, picture galleries, local government, tourist information centres, advertisers, guides, archaeologists and architects (Cano and Mysyk, 2004; Smith, 2004). Meanwhile, people are not only influenced by their culture but they construct it, build it, elaborate it with different strategies according to their needs and circumstances (Kiriakidis, 2008). Through cultural tourism local traditional activities are modernized and preserved and traditional crafts revive (MacDonald and Jolliffe, 2003). When cultural tourism is developed, the accessibility of an area is improved and development projects are encouraged which benefit the local community (Cano and Mysyk, 2004; Smith, 2004). Meanwhile, tourism serves to preserve artifacts for promotion in place marketing (Hall and Jenkins, 1995) but also uses features of myth as collective symbols for establishing identity (Hall and Jenkins, 1995).

Chapter 3

METHODOLOGICAL APPROACHES

Both qualitative and quantitative research methodology can be employed for the triangulation of the results. A diverse range of sources were researched. 'Triangulation' enables the researchers to have a mixture of sources for gathering data and thus "gain a better assessment of the validity of the explanations" (Maxwell, 1996: 75-76). Since most instruments are not as accurately desired, the use of multiple measures of the same construct pointing information in the same direction, allows for a better interpretation since different sources of evidence are used for the presentation of findings (Yin, 1993: 69). The multiple sources of evidence provided multiple ways of measuring the same phenomenon. One source may provide the cross reference for the other sources and supplements information from different angles about the general question of inquiry Besides, when the same procedures are followed reliability may be accomplished (Yin, 1993). It is the credibility that is searched in qualitative research; convergence of a major theme or pattern provides credibility to the findings (Maykut and Morehouse, 1994: 146; Robson, 1993: 404). Calvert (1991: 121) and Forster (1994: 155) stated the issue of authenticity that the researchers should deal with in order to verify whether the data are genuine (Kavoura and Bitsani, 2014).

The abovementioned methodology was also employed for the presentation of the distinctive heritage of a country-related to issues of reinforcing its perceived identity, economic and political processes and underscores questions of the power of the state at national and international levels. World Heritage properties nominated to the World Heritage List (List) -a List where properties of outstanding universal value can be inscribed according to the Convention concerning the Protection of the World Cultural and Natural Heritage (Convention). The Convention is an international agreement adopted by the general conference of UNESCO in 1972 where States Parties that have ratified the Convention (they are referred to as 'States Parties' by the Convention) may nominate heritage to the List (Kavoura, 2001; Kavoura and Bitsani, 2013). Similar methodology has been followed in the examination of the city of Trieste, Italy which examined the formation of intercultural relations and the role of organizational networks in the Mediterranean and in Europe which consist of the basic body of the so called Greek commercial dispersion; cultural interactions emerged as a result of these networks (Bitsani and Kavoura, 2011).

In addition, quantitative methodology was employed with the gathering of questionnaires in order to examine the point of view of the residents or visitors of different places in regard to place marketing issues (Bitsani and Kavoura, 2014 for the role of the host community in Istria, Croatia; Kavoura and Katsoni, 2013 on the way visitors decide to visit a place associated with religious tourism in Arcadia, Greece or Bitsani and Kavoura (2013) for the choices of visitors in mountainous Nafpaktia, Greece).

For our research, we adopted the method of the case study as the research strategy in order to examine the procedure of marketing and branding having as a starting point the Rural Tour CADSES (RT) project and going beyond that for many areas, for different peripheries.

In particular, our research for place marketing had an initial focus on the Rural Tour CADSES project and continues with other places aiming through the specific methodology which was developed within the programme and the other case studies not incorporated in the programme to examine the validity and reliability of the methodology and strategic design of place marketing, place branding but also to create a unified model/ proposal for different areas with common characteristics.

In regard to research for places and in marketing research and branding, the boundaries among phenomena and frameworks are not distinct; that is why, the case study or case studies (Yin, 1993) as in this research, seem to be the most appropriate strategy for research (Kavaratzis and Ashworth, 2008). Generalization in case studies is about theoretical propositions not about populations (Yin, 1993; Hartley, 1994: 225) and our aim is to lead our work to the creation of a unified model for the branding of regions. Its innovativeness lies in that it aims to the holistic sustainable development of local communities, via the enhancement of procedures and tools of management, marketing and development within a framework of cooperation of all the parties involved.

Contemporary organizations in local communities which transcend boundaries, management and techniques may employ tools of Information and Communication Technologies (ICTs) which may in fact determine the content and the procedures of social change. The interdependent world we live, suggests that the concept of localization continues to give power to the nation state, to the smaller communities which remain important with their powers of action redefined rather than the argument that globalization heralds the end of the power of smaller entities; ICTs have a role to play which may lead to economic activity and can be a means to reduce social exclusion; they may achieve networks that link the global, the nation state and organizations and bring development in socio-cultural terms (see for example, the case of Egypt, El Sayed and Westrup, 2003: 79). The use of ICTs offer people the ability to make use of them and line to engage in meaningful social practices (Kavoura and Katsoni, 2013).

Under this perspective and for its implementation, apart from the creation of tools of ICTs for the marketing and management of businesses, but also for citizens and representatives of the public sector who participate in the elevation of places, an attitude and a social change is created especially with the use of ICTs and marketing in the everyday life of businesses which produce local products but also networks -among the public and the private sector which can be created (Katsoni and Kavoura)- for the holistic development via a unifying framework of activities (for example, the common development of networks of local products and alternative forms of tourism). Within this framework, the "model of collective activity and action" in regard to the intervention results and the cooperation of partners was methodologically promoted.

More specifically, there is reference to the RT project in Bitsani's and Kavoura's work (2010), which was financed within the European program of transnational cooperation, INTERREG IIIB CADSES, began in June 2006 with the intention of promoting a model for the development, (in sustainable and innovative ways), of an integrated rural tourism in Central Eastern Europe (which uses the acronym area CADSES) http:// europa.eu.int/comm/ agriculture/rur/leaderplus/index_el.htm.

That project promoted rural tourist resources that are on the margin of mass tourism, defined strategic actions that create and promote a network between activities presently in place, providing incentives that stimulate the development of new services (European Committee, 2000). The basic concept underpinning RT methodology is to create synergies between the advertising initiatives conducted by individual companies on the one hand and, on the other, effectively promote the region where these companies are located (territorial marketing), as well as creating a collective mark that identifies shared products, services and activities. Therefore, the intention of the RT project is to satisfy tourists needs, by improving the quality of what the region offers, and at the same time, improve the growth opportunities of rural areas by affirming cultural identity and diversity, thereby valorizing the local oenological-gastronomical products, along with the human and economic resources of a region (Bitsani and Panagou in Bitsani and Kavoura, 2010).

The insufficient level of the promotion of environmental, cultural and landscape resources, the difficulty in accessing rural areas, and the shortage of infrastructures and lodgings that are qualified to accommodate tourism, are among the main causes of why marginal regions are not influenced by the active benefits brought by the tourism in neighboring areas (Lytras, 2005). On the other hand, the success of the initiatives connected to rural tourism requires a long term financial and environmental sustainability. This long term financial sustainability can by realised if, subsequent to an initial investment, the tourist initiatives are capable of generating a positive flow of funds to ensure an enduring success of the initiative itself (Bitsani and Kavoura, 2010).

Alternatively, environmental sustainability is connected with the capability of increasing the economic value of the natural and cultural patrimony by adopting a tourism proposal that does not damage the same patrimony. High revenues can be realized both by directing a greater number of tourists to the interested regions, and by protracting their presence in the low season (Bitsani and Kavoura, 2010). The RT project allows the pursuit of such an objective by first realizing a marketing plan along with certain guide lines for a sustainable rural tourism, and second, by applying these in the pilot zones identified within the involved regions. Additionally, the project provides the possibility of creating a recognizable mark that clearly identifies the initiatives of a sustainable rural tourism, based on rules and operating procedures that form the conditions for the attribution of the mark itself and for the subsequent certification process. The RT project involved a partnership comprising five public institutions belonging to four State members of the European Union (Italy, Hungary, Poland, Austria) and one outside EU (Croatia). In particular, the six institutions that participated in the project were:

- Region of Veneto– the Office for Integrated Tourist Promotion (Italy)
- Region of Emilia Romagna– Tourism Service (Italy)
- Region of Opolskie (Poland)
- Federal State of Carinthia (Austria)

- Micro-Regional Development Association of Szıcsıny Area (Hungary)
- AZRRI - Agency for Rural Development of Istria Ldt. Pazin (Croatia) (Bitsani and Kavoura, 2010).

TERRITORIAL MARKETING ACCORDING TO THE RT METHODOLOGY

Territorial marketing based on the tourist potential of an area is an effective instrument of socio-economic development through the promotion and the evaluation of the tourist resources of the area. Place marketing is described as activities "designed to create favorable dispositions and behavior toward geographic locations" (O' Leary and Iredal in Braun, Kavaratzis and Zenker, 2010: 2). The goal is to achieve a quick and consistent increase in its ability to attract an influx of tourists (Bitsani and Kavoura, 2010).

The territorial marketing plan provided the promotion and the exploitation of the tourism resources present in the area, for the purpose of obtaining a rapid and considerable increase in the capacity to attract those tourists who are interested in discovering the landscape, historical, cultural and oenologic-gastronomic richness that is typical of Eastern Europe. An essential element of a region's promotion that was both coherent and effective, was the active participation of the local "actors" (public authorities, associations and enterprises) (Bitsani and Kavoura, 2010).

The system of governance promoted by the project activities encouraged the participation of public authorities belonging to different institutional levels (Region, Province, Mountain Communities and Municipalities), in concomitance with private economic "actors" and specific associations that were present in the region. The promotion of the region required adopting an approach of implemented actions that started with the exigencies and necessities felt as more urgent by the locals (bottom–up approach). This led to an involvement and an active participation in the process of realizing the project by all the local public institutions, and by the representative associations and private enterprises. Such partnerships were developed through a series of meetings starting in June 2007. The in-depth knowledge of the region and its particularities allowed the local actors (Municipality, Companies, Wine and Typical Products Roads, products protection Consortium, tourism promotion Consortium), to have a fundamental role in creating the on-line system of research about tourism resources. These participants furnished information and data that are interesting for surveying precious tourist resources that are largely unknown by most tourists (Bitsani and Kavoura, 2010).

Within this framework and in order for the aim of development to be accomplished via tourism as the sustainable form of region development and peripheries, the change of the image of these regions was of outmost significance; we argue that this may take place via their branding based on the same methodology as mentioned above, and having as a goal the elevation of the identity of a region and the cooperation of local forces of a place in order to promote its distinct characteristics (Cassel, 2008).

In that way, we argue that a double result is accomplished since on the one hand, when regions operate in synergy and cooperation to promote their brand, in a systemic way and one complementary to the other within networks, then, multiple results are created for the 'emerging' entity which includes and incorporates them all (see for example Kavoura and Katsoni, 2013 who argue for the creation of networks that could raise tourism inflows and the incorporation of places in Greece associated with religious tourism, creating a religious associated network for Greece as a tourist religious destination; this latter will also elevate the brand identity of Greece as a point of reference of Orthodox Christianity; tourists can then be segmented based on their preferences -for example, religious heritage tourism aimed at the Russian Orthodox tourists (Kavoura, 2013). In addition, the access to a place's heritage, distinct characteristics, associated with its place identity is improved (Mitsche et al., 2013: 68); residents but also visitors and potential visitors on the basis of a common identity, have common elements to share and the sense of "we" can be accomplished, their identification with the place (each one identified himself or part of himself with it); in that way, the necessary social cohesion can be enhanced (Bitsani and Kavcoura, 2011). The necessary social change can be accomplished with the use of ICTs (Katsoni, 2011) towards the creation of dynamic conditions and progress for local communities, elements which may guarantee their sustainability in the contemporary complex and instable environment of gloabalizaiton and of big economic crisis. The process suggested by the RT methodology in order to carry out a territorial marketing plan, is divided into the phases described in the next section.

DEVELOPMENT OF AN OPERATING PLAN
FOR TERRITORIAL/PLACE MARKETING

The territory/place in reference is the geographical and administrative area which is interested in implementing a plan of tourist development and territorial marketing. The dimensional scale of such an area can range from a town (or towns) to a province (or provinces) (Bitsani and Kavoura, 2010).

The development of the operating plan constitutes: i) planning a series of activities related to advertising communication ii) territorial intervention in order to increase the quantity of information available to the visitors iii) public relation activities and finally iv) involvement of the public sector (local administrations) and of the private sector (trade associations) in order to involve the local communities interested in the plan.

The results of the analysis of tourist potential are then used to develop a S.W.O.T. matrix -where S stands for Strengths, W for Weaknesses, O for Opportunities and T for Threats as has been discussed in Chapter 2 -an instrument which to identify concrete actions to be carried out during the execution of the territorial marketing plan, with the final aim of increasing tourist influx to the area.

The operating plan is implemented in the territory in reference and the results of the actions are collected and examined on the basis of predefined indicators (Key Performance Indicators). These data are then used, in a feedback cycle, in order to improve the plan itself and its subsequent implementation. Appropriate questionnaires are distributed to visitors of the respective area, in order to evaluate the degree of satisfaction with their visit, the quality of services, the media and communication strategies that inform them about the specific place and its distinct characteristics in order to be competitive and attract tourists (Kavoura and Katsoni, 2013; Papp and Raffay, 2011). Moreover, independent audits can be commissioned about the structures which are responsible for the application of the plan.

Chapter 4

PLACE IDENTITY/NATIONAL IDENTITY: THE IMAGE OF THE PLACE AND PLACE BRAND

Landscape is the area which surrounds us and the world in which we live, a synthesis of human areas, or those that have been altered from the human factor, which is used as the basis or framework for our collective existence (Jackson, 1984: 40-43). Thus, our life, is closely related with the concept of place, yet, this concept has different meanings for each person.

The search of the concept of place accompanied the development of geography in the Anglo-Saxon areas in the 20th century. The search of the definition of cultural landscape is associated with the influence of a group of people over a natural setting (Sauer, 1984: 19-31). Apart from the existence of a landscape as a human entity, Sauer also elevated such definition as a conceptual meaning for geography to describe "an austere geographical way of view of human culture" (Sauer, 1984: 33-54).

The cultural landscape is not only defined based on specific material (tangible) elements, but is also based on symbolic elements, which express a specific system of meanings, senses, values through space, such as religious symbols, social institutions, cultural specificities, economic activities and relations (Kavoura, 2013; Mitsche et al., 2013). Thus, a place is tangible which is universally accepted; a place which is understood by people or is transformed based on people's means, wishes and aims; a general framework of life, which reveals history and different aspects of life, based on the socio-economic conditions and the cultural system. In regard to its territorial boundaries, the place is defined from the field of operation of human senses and relations.

Therefore, should places always change since our way of life changes? or should a place keep the best, the most representative, the most interesting of the cultural achievements of past while, at the same time, controlled changes can be made and from whom? Social and cultural issues in the promotion of a place, a country and its distinctive elements are usually left unsaid, hidden socio-political implications exist and these issues are usually left unexamined (Kavoura, 2001; Kavoura, 2007; Konečnik, 2004) although nowadays, places, urban or rural, experience changes all over the world.

Both urban but also rural places are significant, especially those which have been characterized and identified with important sites of the past and mainly recognized because of these. This condition made us think about the role of historic and ancient monuments and heritage in general for the recognizability of the place but also of other intangible elements which may contribute to such recognizability and access (Mitsche et al., 2013). Thus, all these elements constitute the place identity, whether this is a city, a country, a territory, rural or semi-urban place. Place identity which incorporates values, myths, way of life, festivities, traditions, is part of the national identity of a population and is interrelated with it; it is this identity that is projected to the world via the promotional material in print or electronic form (Kavoura, 2013) promoting in that way, tourism to a region, a place, a country.

Thus, at this point we need to develop the theoretical argument around the concept of national and cultural place identity and areas in general. Initially, the concept of national identity emerged in the 19th century where the concept of nation state prevailed and nation states were the only known political structures /entities.

The fundamental characteristics of a national identity are a historic territory, common myths and historical memories, a common, mass public culture, a common economy and common legal rights and duties are acknowledged as being parts of the national identity of a population but also a common economoy with the possibility of mobility of the members within its territorial boundaries of the ocmmunity (Smith, 1991:8-15, Smith, 1996: 447; Gellner, 1983: 49, 125). Identity is defined in a distinct way for each population. Heritage can be part of the national identity. Heritage is a broad area which incorporates many aspects and meanings which may vary. Nature, prehistory, archaeological remains, buildings, religion, language, traditions, and folklore all symbolise the past and are worth retaining for future generations. These variables, which are incorporated into the heritage definition, may be distinguished as material and immaterial, tangible and intangible, physical or social forms of heritage (Zeppel and Hall, 1991;

Lowenthal, 1994; Nuryanti, 1996; Kavoura, 2001; Mitsche et al., 2013). Sites are part of the national identity and they are manifestations and signifiers of the iconography of nationhood offering a sense of continuity and belonging for a population (Smith, 1991: 77; Feilden and Jokilehto, 1993: 77; Pritchard and Morgan, 2001; Kavoura, 2001).

Nevertheless, supranational legislation which comes from entities such as the European Union, but also the procedures of globalization make the concepts of the nation and the national identity less discrete than in the past. Nevertheless, the country, common myths and historic memories such as the common culture remain to prevail as characteristics of national identity (Dinnie, 2008: 112-113). Thus, the concept of localization may give power to the nation state or even to small regions which remain important and significant (El Sayed and Westrup, 2003: 79); this is due to the fact that the state loses its role and thus, people come closer to their place identity which is in line with national identity. The glocalization of governance which brings social disempowerment and a growing influence and power for regional economic elites is argued to be the case (Braun, Kavaratzis and Zenker, 2010: 3).

That is why collaborative planning for the recognizability of the place and its attractiveness may put much more emphasis on the inclusion of all stakeholders in the process of the promotion of a place (Cassel, 2008). Stakeholders' participation is significant; the role of key people in charge may mobilize the presentation of specific identity elements and specific characteristics (Kuscer, 2013; Kavoura, 2001) as is the case for Greece (Kavoura, 2001: 132); the promotion of Denmark (Ooi, 2004) or India (Kerrigan, Shivanandan and Hede, 2012) to name but a few. Positive aspects of the place or destination can be then institutionalized, asserting the place's uniqueness which may put emphasis on the historical, cultural and social values of society (Kavoura, 2001; Ooi, 2004: 112).

Cultural elements of national identity can be the language, literature, music, sport or architecture Culture as a constituent element of cultural identity may thus be characterized as non- tangible element of every population and every country and is the result of every human action. That is why, the concept national can be associated with place identity. Thus, nations and regions have via symbols of their culture the possibility of renegotiating, of constructing and advertising their identity since symbols of culture can be the economic and legal systems, religious convictions or culture (Dinnie, 2008: 111, 118; Skinner and Kubacki, 2007: 308-309).

To this end, the role of media and advertising campaigns is significant; people's willingness to travel more and spend money, while the travel costs have decreased, the effort made by destinations to become distinct and avoid homogeneity, the demand for cultural products, lead places to be competitive and promote their uniqueness (Papp and Raffay, 2011; Vinieratou et al., 2007: 27-28). Thus, research on place branding incorporates issues related to policy design and implementation issues, to issues as to what consists of identity for a place but also to the management of places as destinations.

PLACE IDENTITY WITHIN THE FRAMEWORK OF TOURISM

The initial concept of the idea of place branding comes from dealing with regions as destinations which should have an image in order to consist of poles of tourism attraction. Later, the concept of destination was specialized in order to include many forms of geographical entities such as a nation, a region, a city, even an event or / and a tourist resort. It could be argued that the relation which develops among the terms that refer to place branding, destination branding and nation branding is the following: the first two terms, relate with each other based on a general to specific perspective, the first being a conceptual term and the latter, putting emphasis on the tourism sector. Further, the term destination branding, may be analyzed in more specific forms of branding, based on the geographical entity which every time consists of the subject under management, one of which is nation branding (Hanna and Rowley, 2008: 61-64).

Nevertheless, it was realized that that the concept of place is complex and demands more holistic approaches since the area of tourism with which it may cooperate and is associated with, is not isolated, on the contrary, it is very much related to cultural and historic apporaches (Anholt, 2005: 118). The tourism industry uses features of myth as collective symbols of a place's, a country's distinctiveness and these myths help to construct national identity in the imagination of the visitor (Lowenthal, 1994: 49; Palmer, 1999: 316; Kavoura, 2001: 68).

NATION BRAND AND NATION BRANDING

In the creation of a brand, certain key elements connect which include the product and its abilities, the brand and its name, the brand symbolism and imagery and the consumer (Meenagham, 1995: 25).

Brand is also associated with intangible elements and attributes existing in the imagination of the customer (Kapferer, 2013: 27; Kim, 1990). Branding has been considered a potent marketing tool defined as selecting a consistent element mix to identify and distinguish (a destination) through positive image-building containing unique identity; the goal is to build and manage a desirable image that can attract tourists -when we talk about destinations- or customers -when we refer to products- and to differentiate one's destination or a product from competitors (Park and Petrick, 2008: 262; Anholt, 2007: 4) incorporating all the agents involved, consisting in that way, a holistic approach (Anholt, 2005: 117). The elements of differentiation, the distinct characteristics of a place -tangible and intangible (Mitsche et al., 2031)- which also associate a place with its target groups can be the place's brand (Dinnie, 2008: 15). Tourists acquire knowledge from their own experiences, those of others and visual and sensory stimuli, all of which educate them about destination image; destination image is formed from communication inputs throughout one's lifetime and tourists retain messages that are relevant to them (Molina and Esteban, 2006: 1039; Kavoura, 2013: 72). Countries, nations places are called to manage this image to be in line with the visitors's and all the agents involved point of view.

Nation branding refers to the application of branding and marketing communications techniques to promote and manage a nation's image; thus a nation's brand may be considered the desired image (Dinnie, 2008). Nations shape and reshape their identities or according to Olins (2002: 3) rebrand themselves because their reality changes and they project this change to their audiences. A nation's brand is what a nation's people want the world to understand about their nation and seeks to incorporate its most central, enduring and distinctive features (Scott et al., 2011). Branding the nation in the globalised world is a strategy or tool in the competition for attention and wealth, as well as a tool of self-affirmation as is the case with the formation of the Chinese national identity (Scott et al., 2011: 227). Thus, it is typical that the communication methods that marketing and advertising employs -for example, the official narrative of a state in relation to branding a nation- would include the most representative elements as part of its identity. The incorporation of all the agents involved and their connection in order to develop public, private and social networks and the necessary synergies in a place should take place keeping in mind the public interest which will be later discussed.

PLACE BRANDING AND PLACE MARKETING – AN INTERCONNECTED RELATIONSHIP

The concept of brand has four different dimensions, the development of which will be broadly attempted to be related with the concept under consideration of place brand. In particular, the first one is brand identity and is related to the identity, the core, which in the case of consumer goods is what is seen in the consumers' eyes, that is, the slogan, the framework, the wrapping (Anholt, 2007: 5-6). The concept of brand identity has as a further aim, that is, the differentiation of one product and its placement in a competitive environment (Hankinson, 2004: 110). In the case of regions, this is the regional (local) brand identity and in the case of nations, it is called the national brand identity.

Nonetheless, in order for the identity of a place to be transformed to a commercial, brand identity, we need to accept beforehand that the latter will be only formed on the basis of a limited number of constitutive elements of the first, that is why, these need to be carefully chosen beforehand, based on the criterion of satisfying the strategy of place marketing and place branding (Dinnie, 2008: 45-46) both from the tangible and intangible elements that a place may have (Mitsche et al., 2013; Kavoura, 2013). Following, the second dimension is the brand image and is associated with the belief that exists for a brand in the mind of the consumers; it is associated with the image a product has and at times, but not always, it may be associated with the identity of a product (Anholt, 2007: 5-6). For example, a history of conflict and division associated with the city of Belfast, can provide the platform for future aspiration and change (Northover, 2010).

Its third dimension refers to the brand purpose and consists of the equivalent of the internal image of a business. It is based on the idea that every effort made from the company's point of view will not bring the anticipated results if it is not supported from the human resources and the other stakeholders of the business and that the combination of a powerful internal culture with a dynamic external feature, may create a very powerful brand. Such view of the concept of brand may be effectively used in the case of regions and countries and have special significance (Anholt, 2007: 5-6). In regard to a place brand, destination stakeholders include public sector and governments, such as National Tourism Organizations, residents, tourism industry sector, destination management organization and other groups-such as the most important categories which may influence and determine the management and marketing (Goeldner and Ritchie in Konečnik, 2004).

Last but not least, the fourth dimension of brand is associated with brand equity and refers to the value that positive image has for a business, which may be stronger than its material elements. Such a view may be also adopted in the case of regions and countries; its presence may bring economic benefits for a periphery or a place or a country (Anholt, 2007: 5-6; Kavoura and Bitsani, 2013).

Apart from this definitional approach, there is also the approach which departs from the consumer perspective approach and refers to the ability of the consumer to recognise the brand, to make judgements regarding quality, uniqueness, fame and other elements. Of determining significance for the concept of brand equity, under the consumer perspective, is also the concept of brand loyalty, which, refers to the devotion to the brand. In regard to the content of this concept in the business sector, this is associated with the fact that when there is devotion this leads to a high degree of sentimental consumer connection with a brand. The realization of such an aim is considered for a business more preferrable to the repeated simple purchase of a product (Anholt, 2007: 5-6).

The abovementioned, adopted in place branding may mean that: for the brand equity concept, regions located within countries but also countries themselves, with abundance of symbols and imaginative correlations, have the uniqueness under search and a distinct iconography, as a result of their local/ national identity, which reinforces the development of the brand of a country; national identity can be related with branding if the perceived distinct elements of a nation are promoted and are embedded with special emphasis and symbolism (Kavoura, 2013: 72) and a country's culture consists of part of its national identity. In regard to brand loyalty, the cultural elements and the resources that places and countries have and the meanings these bring about to people, may create strong feelings (Kavoura and Stavrianea under review). In that way, a place or a country may promote its unique characteristics, its unique elements, the unique selling proposition, to use marketing terms. This may be enhanced taking into consideration that visitors may build their own itinerary, they may seek attractions they are familiar with; such attractions may draw attention to the place when they are also associated with popular events, recognized tourist attractions or well tested types of attractions so that visitors can choose from an active canvassing in the end (Ooi, 2011: 188). There is relation between the trust and brand loyalty (Christou, 2004) and the role of people as visitors, recipients and co-creators of place branding is further discussed in the next Chapter.

Chapter 5

EXTERNAL PUBLIC/TOURISM AND TOURISM BEHAVIOR: DEFINING 'EXPERIENCE'

Place marketing and branding is influenced from its recipients, in other words, the consumers, rather visitors of the place which are called to buy the tourist product, to become consumers of the region and its residents for a specific period in time. The aim is the visitors to become loyal and with the experience of tourism to visit the place, the region, the area again and become a favourite destination, but also to advertise it to other people and to convince them to visit it consisting in that way, the most significant ambassadors since the word of mouth from relatives and friends is considered to be very important to the decisions made (Brakus et al., 2009; Andersson and Ekman, 2009). In other words, people can be active partners and co-producers of public goods and services (Braun, Kavaratzis and Zenker, 2010).

In addition, via the psychological and sentimental processes that the experience causes -as it is further analyzed in the Chapter, people can feel part of an 'imagined community' -a sense of coherence that exists between community members who feel a sense of belonging to the same group, even if they have never met (Anderson, 1991); they identify with the specific place identity which consists of an extension of the community people live within the boundaries, natural and administrative of the place. New technologies, advertising media and social networks in the digital environment contribute to such identification and feedback so that "experiences can also occur …when consumers are exposed to advertising and marketing communications, including Web sites" (Brakus et al, 2009: 53); thus, experience is kept alive even if this refers to people who share ideas all over the world.

While research has focused on contributing factors influencing people's choices on vacations and the reasons tourists select one or the other destination

(Bitsani and Kavoura, 2013; Bitsani and Kavoura, 2012), studies on the influence and the role of experiences are still limited (Brakus et al., 2009) and even for the conceptualization and measurement of loyalty in the service context there is still disagreement on how loyalty is formed (Bennett and Rundle Thiele; 2004; Stavrianea, 2010), not to mention that studies on destination loyalty are still lacking (Yuksel, Yuksel and Bilim, 2010) and authors have called for research on the implementation of contemporary marketing constructs in order to be able to operationalize and measure the concept of the imagined community in relation to them (Kavoura and Katsoni, 2013).

People have unique characteristics and in that way, people with similar characteristics may consist of a whole, a specific tourist market which may interest the destination country or place. Communicating an idea to a group or a community is made easier when "the idea is part of the very fabric of group life... is a notion that is already passively a part of the normative structure of the group" (Fine, 1981: 95). Such a group shares characteristics that are typical to this group based on the typology they belong; for example, Bitsani's and Kavoura's (2012) research examined the motivations for attending wine festivals in the region of Veneto, Italy in an attempt to relate gastronomical and wine tourism and specify tourists' typology. Results showed that different categories for gastroenological visitors exist who share different characteristics and could be appropriately targeted with the implementation of an advertising communication programme which may promote information about the area and its wineries specifically targeted on these typologies and based on their specificities.

Nevertheless, we should take into consideration that even if we discuss the fact that a place may attract different typlogies of visitors, all share a common element: they are associated with the significance of the image of a place and its identity, its distinct characteristics in relation to experiences visitors may share. Brand experiences are subjective, internal consumer responses (sensation feelings, cognitions and behavioral responses evoked by many different stimuli which occur when the consumer gets into contact with the brand in a direct (physical experience) or in an indirect (virtual presentation or in an advertisement) way (Brakus et al., 2009: 52-53; Kavoura and Stavrianea, under review). Thus, the brand experience for a place is significant and may consist of the key for the strategic planning of place branding and place marketing nowadays.

Although the concept of experience has been examined by authors, it is mainly examined in the sector of services' provision where consumers receive service; it is a business approach where memorable experiences are associated with economic offer, in which the consumer also participates at a personal level (Pine and Gilmore, 1999: 53-66; Skinner, 2008; Brakus et al., 2009: 52). Brand experiences may also occur in place brands (Skinner, 2008).

The creation of memorable experiences is considered to be a deliberate strategy of businesses and tourism packages, in order to attract individual consumers and visitors (Bitsani and Kavoura, 2014). Experience is basically of personal and subjective character, while it exists in the person's soul (Brakus et al., 2009). As a result, the person has a decisive and significant role to play in the way experiences take place and influence the decisions made for a place. The association of brand experience with the role of place identity in leading to tourists' satisfaction and loyalty intentions will provide marketers and policy makers with informed decisions regarding planning and marketing in a tourism destination (Kavoura and Stavrianea under review).

DIMENSIONS OF EXPERIENCE ASSOCIATED WITH A PLACE BRAND

Narrations as a tool for the creation of value to a place and the expectation that the consumer or visitor will experientially participate may integrate a place, a city, a region into stories and interpretation procedures regarding narration, may improve access to the destination (Mitsche et al., 2013; Kavoura, 2007). Stories fascinate people; they have power and can be used in branding (Lundqvist et al., 2013).

Kavoura and Stavrianea (under review) argue for the significance that brand experience may have in order for consumers to make choices for a place while limited research has been done on the nature and dimensional structure of brand experiences, the experiences provided by brands (Brakus et al., 2009).

Brakus et al. (2009) distinguish four dimensions of brand experience: affective, behavioral, sensory and intellectual experiences. Kavoura and Stavrianea (under review) apply the four experiential dimensions of Brakus et al. (2009) in the tourism context, in relation to a place brand. Place brand experience may include intellectual experience that can stimulate a visitor's curiosity to learn more about a place brand. Place brand experiences also refer to the ability of the brand to engage consumers' convergent/analytical and divergent/ imaginative thinking (Zarantonello and Schmitt, 2010). Consumers may use convergent thinking to analyze different messages about a destination or use divergent thinking about potential experiences they may have in a destination sometimes stimulated by slogans, web sites and other media communications (Brakus et al., 2009), or other heuristics, used by marketers that appeal to their needs (Kavoura and Stavrianea under review).

In regard to the dimension of sensory brand experiences, this includes aesthetic and sensory qualities such as visual, auditory, tactile, gustative and olfactory stimulations; the behavioral dimension includes bodily experiences, lifestyles and interactions with the brand (Zarantonello and Schmitt, 2010).

Affective brand experiences include feels and moods evoked by a brand and emotions; these dimensions have been examined by Brakus et al. (2009), who in their initial research have also associated brand experiences with a social context for example, "membership in an exclusive, country-clubbish community, part of a smarter community" (Brakus et al. 2009: 55), nonetheless, this latter needs further analysis (Brakus et al., 2009: 57) which allows space to make inferences with the connection of branded experience with Anderson's theory on the 'imagined community' (Kavoura and Stavrianea under review).

The satisfaction that a visitor enjoys, for example at a rural tourism unit, is influenced not only from the accommodation but also from factors which are associated with the area as a whole and the stages before and after visiting it (see for example research on the mountainous Nafpaktia, Greece, Bitsani and Kavoura 2013). The provision of information for visiting these areas is significant for visitors to get informed about the area although relatively little research has been made (Dodd, 1999; Lytras, 2005; Vlachvei, Notta and Ananiadis, 2009).

In other words, experiences offered to the potential visitors but also to visitors of a place need to match with their preferences (for example, religious heritage tourism associated with Orthodoxy in Greece, aimed at the Russian tourists (Kavoura, 2013: 81). These experiences may be associated with the core of a country's brand; the country's, the place's, the region's brand must incorporate the spirit of its target groups -which may be diverse groups such as tourists that this Chapter examined but they may also be students, investors, residents, foreign governments that a country for example, is trying to attract and/ or negotitate with (Gilmore, 2002; Gow and Bellou, 2003). This will be discussed in the next chapters.

Chapter 6

THE ROLE OF THE IMAGINED COMMUNITY IN PLACE MARKETING

Anderson's theory of the imagined community (1991) is based on the distinct elements of a population which bring them together. Anderson's imagined community is the "politically bounded community where a sense of coherence exists between its members who feel a sense of belonging to the same group even if they have never met" (Anderson, 1991: 6-7). Anderson has discussed the belief of a people in their distinctiveness with the terminology of the imagined community where a sense of coherence exists between its members who feel a sense of belonging to the same group (Anderson, 1991) as has been mentioned. It may create a sense of place which may reinforce an emotional link with a specific destination and its unique attributes which incorporate both tangible and intangible elements (Kavoura and Katsoni, 2013).

Place marketing is associated with tangible and intangible characteristics; religious buildings for example, are part of the tangible elements of a place, while religion can be part of its intangible elements. Rainisto (2003) argued for the critical success factors in place marketing utilized for place development where a clustering of like industries, a geopolitical physical space or a nation-state is incorporated among the definitions of the place (Kotler et al. in Rainisto, 2003: 11). "The physical and material aspects of a destination, called tangibles, include ...religious buildings, churches and especially monasteries...the intangible qualities of a destination include such things as ...tradition, religion..." (Mitsche et al., 2013: 69). These religious sites and intangible qualities may be connected with the identity of a population and create a sense of place (Mitsche et al., 2013: 68-69).

This sense of place is enhanced if people -including visitors- have cultural familiarity with the destination while at the same time, regional communities can identify and relate to it (Mitsche et al., 2013: 69). Place attachment incorporates place identity-dimensions of the self that define the individual's personal identity in relation to the physical environment- and place dependence -the provision of amenities which are essential for the desired actions (Kyle et al., 2004: 124) although there is limited research and authors call for research since destination authorities and marketers may make informed decisions regarding the marketing of a place taking into consideration people's feelings and possible bonds with the place (Yuksel, Yuksel and Bilim, 2010: 274; Kavoura and Stavrianea under review).

Personal knowledge and experience as mentioned by Mitsche et al. (2013: 68-69) via cultural heritage -such as religious sites- may create images and imaginations in people's minds; these sites may then create a sense of place; this sense of place is enhanced if the tourists have cultural familiarity with the destination (Mitsche et al., 2013: 69).

Therefore, the more familiarity, sense of closenessness or experiences the consumer, person, visitor has for a destination, the more attached he/she may be with it and involved; involvement "reflects the degree to which a person devotes him or herself to an activity or associated product" (Kyle et al. 2004: 125). A person's involvement is influenced from centrality -how central is an activity, a setting in the individual's life; centrality refers to friends, or others and social interactions centred on the activity, a place or region with which a person may emotionally attach (Kyle et al., 2004: 125, 136). Information about the place to attract people's interest can then be narrated to the people.

As has already been mentioned in the previous Chapter, stories fascinate people, they have power and can used in branding (Lundqvist et al. 2013). It is not only significant to identify the 'important', distinct characteristics of a place, as part of its DNA, but also construct powerful narratives that create meanings (Hjortegaard Hansen, 2010: 268). Feelings about a place can be created from the residents of a community, a city, a region over time especially through enactment and participation in public rites -which may leave, as literature has suggested, a small emotional trace, local public emotions- and local authorities have a word to say in such procedure (Smith and Darlington, 2010). The local narratives of a place which project the identity of a place, its specificities and particularities are significant in successful place branding, -see for example the narratives for the island of Santorini, Greece (Lichrou, O'Malley and Patterson, 2010) or Scotland's creation of a sense of place with the use of national identity elements for marketing the place as a destination (Durie, Yeoman and McMahon-Beattie, 2006).

Countries, cities, regions promote their distinct characteristics in an attempt to define and differentiate themselves in the competition for attracting tourists and brand themselves; a nation's brand is what a nation's people want the world to understand about their nation and seeks to incorporate its most central, enduring and distinctive features and place branding may become a powerful tool (Scott et al., 2011; Alonso and Bea, 2012). These promoted distinct features may be part of the national identity of a population.

A place's brand identity is closely linked to studies of national identity, which is itself closely linked to the concept of a nation's cultural and political identity (Skinner and Kubacki, 2007). That is why place identity is closely related to national identity. A historic territory, common myths and historical memories, a common, mass public culture, a common economy and common legal rights and duties are acknowledged as being parts of the national identity of a population (Smith, 1991: 8-15, Smith, 1996: 447; Gellner, 1983: 49, 125). Identity is defined in a distinct way for each population. Kirby (1993) referred to New Zealand where bio-system is presented as part of a unique national heritage and a strong indicator of the country's identity (Morgan and Pritchard, 2002).

Heritage, related to natural or cultural aspects may be used to differentiate one country from another; it is the significance of this heritage that is acknowledged by New Zealanders themselves and other countries as the destination brand (Morgan and Pritchard, 2002) in the above mentioned example and brand represents the core values of a destination (Gilmore, 2002: 285). Branding aims to explore ways to add value to the basic product or service and thus, create brand preference and loyalty (Kavaratzis and Ashworth, 2008). "Natonal identity can be related with branding if the perceived distinctive elements of a nation are promoted and embedded with special emphasis and symbolism" (Kavoura, 2013: 72).

Based on Anderson's imagined community theory, who argued for the sense of belonging that may exist among people who have never met, though, they share common elements and feelings (Anderson, 1991), Kavoura and Katsoni (2013) and Kavoura and Stavrianea (under review) argue that there is relation between this distinct theoretical approach of the imagined community with the marketing and tourism consumer behavior discipline, having been examined as this is expressed by religious tourists information search behavior use of tourism distribution channels (Kavoura and Katsoni, 2013). Kavoura and Katsoni (2013) examined the type and extent of the use of tourism distribution channels, provided by the regional state authorities in order to promote an imagined community associated with religion. Case studies for a projected identity from a prefecture at a state regional level (Arcadia, Greece) found to incorporate religion as a typical part of Greek culture, validating results of previous studies that have taken place at a national level in Greece (see the case of the communicating messages through the official narrative for the presentation of the World Heritage Sites that Greece has nominated to the World Heritage List as heritage of outstanding value -Kavoura, 2001; Kavoura, 2007; Kavoura, 2013). These cases illustrated the dependence of the regional and national state in symbolism, alhough the state should function under the rules of equality and rationality -the principles of bureaucracy are associated with rationality and law (Weber in Fopp, 1997). In that way, a place can be promoted to those interested in the specific characteristics and distinct elements on offer that match and suit with their personal interests and the associations one can make with a place, a region, a city, a country.

Kavoura and Stavrianea (under review) argue that place identity is associated with a sense of being a city person, a small-town person, of a country person (Hummon 1986: 3) locating in that way, the self within a specific community which is spatially defined; at the same time, the sense of 'placelessness', the symbolic placement which is not only directly associated with a residential status (Hummon, 1986: 4; Hidalgo and Hernández, 2001) is acknowledged, situating a person in the world, the nation, identifying himself/herself with others, "forging in that way, a sense of belonging and attachment" (Hummon 1986: 4; Hidalgo and Hernández, 2001: 274) portraying the type of person someone is, based on values, interest and knowledge. In that way, people may identify with different forms of community, develop feelings of attachment that they "belong in that kind of community, that they are of this kind of person" (Hummon, 1986: 21), like a city or a nation but not much research has taken place (Hidalgo and Hernández, 2001: 274). Place identity is associated with what the location symbolizes (Yuksel et al., 2010: 276). The role of place identity refers therefore, to a symbolic, emotional and affective attachment which involves bonding and experiences (Mlozi et al., 2013), such as the concept of the imagined community.

Then, a region, a place or a country may seek to research who their target groups are in order to promote and advertise messages that are of high value to them, interest to them, attach to them and associate in that way, the specific region, place or a country with them. Thus, advertising as a message intended at a specific audience from a specific person, state, stakeholder who promotes this message, should have an 'effective community of minds' in order for the message to be received, taking into consideration the prior knowledge of the target group (Kilamby et al., 2013: 49). This community may take place with the use of the myth, yet, this does not mean that "the community is the product of the myth"; rather, the community "filters the myth through experience before turning it into conviction"; the myth allows and contributes to 'bind members together" (Kilamby et al., 2013: 49).

Although the cases studied by Kilamby et al. (2013) are associated with products and brand communities, this has also applications in the promotion of nations as brands as well (Kavoura and Stavrianea, under review). An example can be the officially sanctioned 'promotional narrative' that can be employed to project a symbolic sense of imagining with national identity, enhancing in that way, a collective community (see for example, Greece Kavoura, 2013: 69; Kavoura and Stavrianea, under review). This is where communication and advertising may contribute as useful tools.

Advertising can be a shaper of identities and mediator of meanings, particularly those related to nationality and cultural knowledge (O' Donohoe, 2011). Representations of Ireland for example, from advertising practitioners, continue to operate in the global context with a presentation of a specific identity and notions of nationality for it (O' Boyle, 2011). Advertising promotional material and communication campaigns in media -print, electronic and the use of websites as communication tools (Kavoura, 2007; Kavoura, 2013; Mitsche et al., 2013; Alonso and Bea, 2012) to safeguard a holistic integrated communication approach (Zotos, 2008; Belch and Belch, 2009) -may be used for the promotion of the place. Mass media play an influential role in shaping and reshaping public perceptions, including the images people form or construct of other nations or places (Freeman and Nhung Nguyen, 2012). Advertising those elements as part of the destination branding of a region, may be used either for national reasons in order to connect and bring people who share similar ideas together, but also for socio-economic reasons as part of the promotion of the distinctive and unique elements of the tourism destination (Kavoura, 2013; Kavaratzis and Ashworth, 2008).

A REGION'S PRODUCTS AS ELEMENTS OF ITS IDENTITY AND PLACE IDENTITY - THE CHARACTERISTICS AND THE ROLE OF VISITORS

The Case Study of Wine Tourism, Veneto, Italy

The identity of a place is consisted of many different elements as has been mentioned above, of natural and human environment, of history of culture, of society and its economy. Yet, many times, the identity of a region seems to be confined in its image, which may be more than one, depending on the receiver contributing to the place's brand since brands could be perceived differently by various internal and external parties (Veloutsou, 2008).

A place's identity is associated with the past, the present, is the basis for its future and is the result of a continuous procedure that takes into consideration all natural and human resources and the socio-economic conditions of the specific period. Every component of the identity (tangible, intangible, natural, cultural etc) of the place co-operates to create a unique whole constituting the distinct and compact identity of the place. At times, a cultural heritage of great wealth can be a key factor to enhance the brand image of a place as the study of the city of Bilbao, Spain, with the Guggenheim musuem being the main icon, illustrated (Alonso and Bea, 2012).

Thus, in order for a place to be transformed to a place destination its recognizability in other words, the creation of branding is required as is for example, visiting a place for its world famous wines or its architecture creating a tourist identity. This identity is also called 'competitive brand' and is based on the elements of the place identity (Anholt in Dinnie, 2008: 22). Since regions compete in the arena of tourists, they need to coordinate their policies, their actions and their communicative strategies in those sectors which promote and reinforce their unique and competitive advantage; this is how their image will also be reinfoced, improving and elevating the experiences of the visitors they aim to visit or have visited the place.

The team of the Network for European Communications and Transport Activities Research (NECTAR) claims that, in Western Europe the activities of free time will probably be equivalent to 40% of the oveland transport by 2020 (regarding the kilometres covered) and 60% of the air transport; the raising polymorphism of the way of life will have a reflection on the emergence of new types of special tourism markets which will cater for young people, couples with no kids, pensioners and conference participants; the raising demand of tourism will be more obvious to the South European population where the percentages of participation are relatively low. The free movement within the European Union (E.E.) contributes to the rise of newly retired moving from North to South Europe due to the favourable climate (Masser, Sviden and Wegener, 1992: 43-44; Vinieratou et al. 2007; Bitsani and Kavoura, 2013).

Nowadays, it is typical that standardised and mass tourist packages do not cater for tourists' needs. People realized the problems that could be created by the prevalent model of mass tourism and they were driven to search for alternative forms of tourism (ecotourism, rural tourism, cultural tourism, historic tourism). These forms respect the local community and its visitors and in the mean time, the cultural heritage and the environment. Their aim is to offer vacations to tourists that are interesting, yet educating, while beneficial for the local community and have as a result the viability of the tourist areas. According to the World Tourism Organisation, the concept of the viability of the tourist areas implies that the tourist sources (culture, sites, natural environment) are directed in such a way by the inhabitants and the visitors so that preservation is guaranteed and their function for future generations to come (Bitsani and Kavoura, 2013). That is why the provision of information is necessary especially for alternative forms of tourism which consists of the basic tool for local / peripheral development nowadays, identified with place marketing of destinations and place destination branding.

Since decisions are emotionally and personally important to consumers, recalling and reliving social experiences through product consumption which provide consumers with a moment of pleasure (Hwang, McMillan and Lee, 2003) policy makers and marketers need to understand and take thoughtful decisions regarding who their target group is, which are their characteristics. To this end, Konečnik and Go (2008: 181) suggest that market research needs to take place to specify target groups while a place should take into consideration which the competitors are-mainly rival destinations- and identify its true position in the market; both symbolic and experiential benefits are needed with functional benefits (the product itself) in a destination brand's identity.

The products of a place (herbs, wine, food and recipes to mention but a few) can be part of a place identity and branding. The marketing consultants conceive of local and regional food culture as an invention to reflect urban consumers' ideas of the countryside. In contrast to cultural diplomacy, but not in collision with it, we may talk about gastrodiplomacy where countries promote their cuisine for nation branding; in that way, they may raise the global awareness of their cultures (Rockower, 2012) which developed within the rural tourism framework consisting in our days the basis of a powerful brand and in particular, a brand within the framework of gastrotourism as one of the most dynamic forms and there is a big demand for this form of alternative tourism. In that way, marketing and brand return to the product from where they have initially started -gastrotourism- dealing with it from another point of view and content.

Thus, we should put emphasis on the place of origin and the brand of the product coincides with the brand of the region. A connecting bond of such connection is the culture that has developed around the product and its production, its quality, its uniqueness etc. Nevertheless, the most important element which mobilizes the abovementioned is the experience and the satisfaction that consumers have; they become advertisers and promote this image contributing in that way, to its reinforcement, thus, the reinforcement of the product's brand and the place that produces it. This was also validated via our empirical research for enological and gastronomical tourism in Veneto, Italy (Bitsani and Kavoura, 2012); this region, has many difficulties in developing a special tourist product and brand and thus, place marketing due to the fact that Padova and Venice are located nearby with the two of the most powerful tourist brands of Italy, although different one from the each other as mentioned by Bitsani and Kavoura (2012). Since Veneto, Italy is the most active wine-producing region in Italy with varieties of wine such as Corvine Veronese 35-36%; Rondinella 10-40%, Negrana 10%, Rossignola and / or Barbera and/ or Sanlovese and / or Garganeca up to 15% (Ministero Dello Sviluppo Economico, 2011), one can realize this long term financial sustainability if, subsequent to an initial investment, the tourist initiatives are capable of generating a positive flow of funds to ensure an enduring success of the initiative itself (Bitsani and Kavoura, 2012).

As is mentioned in Bitsani's and Kavoura's study in regard to the abovemneitoned study on Veneto, Italy (Bitsani and Kavoura, 2012), Veneto's tourism economy, which is a rural and agricultural region, tourist spending is lower than the national average; international tourist expenditure equalled 4.2 billion euro in 2008, 2.4% less than in 2007 (Statistics Office of Regione Veneto, 2009). Veneto stands out for its low number of nights spent; expenditure per capita stands at around 425 euro compared with an Italian average of 493 euro. On the contrary, there are high revenues from 'incoming tourism' and make Veneto Italy's leading region in terms of payment balance: 2,778,000 euro in 2008 (Statistics Office of Regione Veneto, 2009). According to the study "L'Osservatorio sul Turismo del Vino" that took place in 2011,

56% of the tourists visiting the area stay one night, 26.5% stay for a week while 15% stay for 4 nights (Citta del Vino, 2011: 31). From the amount of money spent by these tourists, 20,7% is spent on restaurants, 20,2% on products, 17% of the money is spent on wine (Citta del Vino, 2011: 31). Thus, Bitsani and Kavoura (2012) argue that there is potential for raising wine tourism in the region. The amount of money spent on wine and related to wine activities such as participation in wine festivals, can be increased if more promotion takes place for the promotion of wine related activities and the region of Veneto.

The fact that there is scarce information for potential wine visitors in the abovementioned study of Veneto, Italy (Bitsani and Kavoura, 2012), illustrates that the region can provide more information via the communication channels to visitors. In fact, a close connection with Padova and Venice may provide tourists flow from the big urban centres to the rural region. This can be the case for other countries as research has shown for Greece and wine tourism that there is lack of collaboration among the wine and remaining tourism activity as part of parallel activities (Velissariou et al., 2009: 318).

The possibility of increasing knowledge about the wine product are among the factors that positively affect the intentions of potential wine tourists which can be combined and enhanced with the personal tourists' interest in wine (Marzo-Navarro and Pedraja-Iglesias, 2009). In that way, a tourist whether having a strong interest or not in wine may be positively motivated to visit a winery if there is provision of information about the area especially if this information can fit in with his/her own personal interests and make him/her feel that he/she belongs to an imagined community where visitors with the interest in wine meet together (physically in the place or virtually on the internet) reinforcing their own brand, that of the Veneto Wine. The point of view although significant is not the only necessary to make a holistic approach towards branding.

Brand identity is better understood from the supply side perspective "before knowing how we are perceived, we must know who we are" (Konečnik and Go, 2008: 178-179; Ying, 2005). The senders of the message (the authorities and the networks created which is discussed in the next Chapter) must know what it is that they want to project for the region, how the location wants to be known in the outside world (its "brand" or desired reputation); emphasis is on the activities in the region, the brand is live and the experience is presented as if it is real (Konečnik, 2004; Daugstad, 2008); these are further discussed.

Chapter 7

THE ROLE OF SYNERGIES AND LOCAL NETWORKS FOR PLACE BRANDING AND PLACE MARKETING

The development of networks with cooperating agents and agents who potentially may have economic and other benefits from such participation is of the outmost significance (Weidenfeld, William, Butler, 2010). If someone belongs in the team, relationships exist; social networks operate for the benefit of all included. The actors involved manage "the tangible and virtual resources" of the social capital under a coherent and structured way which also supports them emotionally (Thornton, Ribeiro-Soviano and Urbano, 2011: 107-108).

According to the Europe INNOVA Cluster Mapping Project (2008), cluster policies and cluster organizations in Europe were described, both at national and at regional level. "A cluster is a geographically proximate group of interconnected companies and associated institutions in a particular field, linked by commonalities and complementarities" (Europe Innova, 2008: 5). The clusters have a shared proximity based on geography and activities (Europe Innova, 2008: 5) and companies/ businesses involved as part of such a network, synergy or cluster can benefit if they work together.

Local businesses can also be part of a regional planning process (Rainisto, 2003: 77). A drawback in the creation of synergies and networks created is the issue of creativity which is confined in the sense that all the parts involved follow a specific direction based on the decisions of the social capital of the community and there is not so much room for individual agency to allow for free expression and presentation of ideas (http://www.istheory.yorku.ca/socialnetworktheory.htm; Jones, in McGehee et al., 2010: 489).

Networks contribute in branding because it makes it easier to strengthen the identity of a place. Every part of the synergy provides their knowledge and combines their capacities, filling, in that way, the parts of the team. The combination of resources can be adopted via the implementation of the internet. We argue that these synergies or networks may consist of the influential part which has a role to play in the creation and preservation of brand destination of the area.

As has been mentioned in Chapter four, section Place branding & place marketing –an interconnected relationship, destination stakeholders include public sector and governments, residents, tourism industry sector, destination management organizations and other groups-such as the most important categories which may influence and determine the management and marketing (Goeldner and Ritchie in Konečnik, 2004). These groups develop dynamic relations with the aim to cooperate and collaborate rather than compete. The aim is the brand identity to be in the centre where all those involved will take care of its elements "historical, national and cultural relationships" (Konečnik and Go, 2008: 179). The cooperation involves a partnership between the public and private sectors, or the close co-operation between all local suppliers (Konečnik, 2004). Destination Management Organizations have shifted in recent years from pure marketing organisations to public -private bodies who do not only project the identity but also physically change it (Govers, 2005: 50).

Tourism destination marketing needs to take into consideration the socio-cultural, geographical position within specific boundaries, environmental framework of each region and it unique needs and characteristics, its attractiveness (Buhalis, 2000). These elements cannot be influenced by destination managers or marketers. The role of strategic destination managers and marketers lies in builiding up the destination's identity (Cai in Konečnik, 2004).

In fact, we argue that destination managers have the power to make arguments about the geographical position of a destination since destination marketing organizations are associated with politics and their management and lack of action-namely referring to 'politics' and 'paucity' (Pride, 2002) not to mention the limited budget that tourist boards may have. If we talk about countries, the environment of marketing a country includes political interests (Konečnik, 2004; Konečnik and Go, 2008: 182).

When different groups get involved in destination branding though, the difficulty lies in being able to promote a consistent message because perceptions vary for a destination (Park and Petrick, 2006). Nevertheless, we argue that if networks are created from those who have a personal interest in the promotion of a destination (for example, farm houses of a rural region) and all of them follow a consistent way of promoting specific characteristics of a destination in the same way, then, a unique identity can be created for this destination as such.

The creation of synergies can offer the promotion of a consistent whole for the potential tourist who may associate the region that adopts similar ways of promotion as a sacred place, a place which is different, has an order, everything is under control and organised. Synergies between teams can offer effective results for the promotion of an area and co-ordination of agencies' activities (Nylander and Hall, 2005: 24; Carlsen, Liburd, Edwards and Forde, 2008: 70-72) is effective enough. The result is that each part of the synergy provides their knowledge and combines their capacities filling in the parts of the team. If such parts are combined, they bring better results than the individual efforts of every person outside the team (Bitsani, 2006: 99; Marzano and Scott, 2009).

Stakeholders' participation is significant; the role of key people in charge may mobilise the presentation of specific brand elements and specific characteristics based on local elements (Kavoura, 2001; Kuscer, 2013; Sartori, Mottironi and Antonioli, 2012) as is the case for Greece (Kavoura, 2001: 132); the promotion of Denmark (Ooi, 2004) or India (Kerrigan, Shivanandan and Hede, 2012) to name but a few. Positive aspects of the place or destination are institutionalised, asserting the place's uniqueness which may put emphasis on the historical, cultural and social values of society (Kavoura, 2001; Ooi, 2004: 112).

Stakeholders may be residents who are also managers in the region; they become committed to the region's branding and promotional efforts and actively participate to the region's promotion, including themselves to such a branding procedure and presenting themselves as being part of the identity of the region (Kemp, Williams and Mordelon, 2012; Kerrigan, Shivanandan and Hede, 2012; Kuscer, 2013; Sartori, Mottironi and Antonioli, 2012); they feel a strong connection for the promotion of the destination since they actually promote themselves, their businesses, their values, their traditions, their home.

In the case of Istria, Croatia the attitudes of the community which incorporates the entrepreneurs of Istria, Croatia towards the promotion of rural and cultural tourism of the area and the factors which formulate their attitudes was examined (Bitsani and Kavoura, 2014). It was found that realization of the benefits for sustainable tourism development via the creation of a network has not taken place. There is inexistence of networks which would bring all stakeholders involved for the promotion of the region together. Residents who are also businessmen in the area are afraid that local culture is in danger to be distorted or destroyed due to tourism increase (Bitsani and Kavoura, 2014) which is in line with other research (see Haralambopoulos and Pizam, 1996). It is suggested that partnerships and networks is a prerequisite for the approval of the sustainable tourist development of a community. The residents as part of the economic activity of the place need to be incorporated in the process of managing, communicating and advertising the region, realizing the benefits that may exist from such a process. The "consumption and construction of place are simultaneous processes in which both tourists and locals play an active role" (Rakić and Chambers, 2012). By creating networks among the interested parties involved, the personal but also the common interest will be safeguarded and all activities will be more organized and coordinated (Bitsani and Kavoura, 2014).

The abovementioned study of Istria, Croatia, illustrated that although there is potential for an innovative approach that would combine natural and cultural elements as the distinct characteristics of the region, the connecting element that would join the agents involved together is missing -the creation of networks)- or the necessary significance has not been attributed to it. These networks or synergies would be encouraged to take away the fear of the parts involved as these were expressed in the research (Bitsani and Kavoura, 2014) should be put aside. Since the world is facing with conditions of economic crisis and recession and tourism can be the 'heavy industry' for countries and places, local authorities, the public sector in other words, in cooperation with the host community could play a significant role to promote its identity. Povilanskas and Armaitiene (2010) argue that the key to tourism competitiveness for a region, a country, a place is the power actor-networks have for marketing the region.

Within the framework of the enrichment of local cultural elements, the co-operation of the periphery is important with all the structures and organisations of the local government, so as to safeguard the necessary national and European resources for the establishment of the cultural centres and museums, the revival of local customs, the hosting of activities, the gentrification and the preservation of monuments and traditional buildings and the protection of archaeological sites; thus, the local communities and all its residents, the public sector, businesses and entrepreneurs operating in the region -associated with agricultural co-ops or cultural associations-, need to cooperate in order to create a network that would bring sustainable tourism development and cooperation among the agents involved including the host community as well.

CORPORATE RELATIONS AND RELATIONSHIP BUILDING AS A BASIS OF PLACE BRANDING AND PLACE MARKETING STRATEGY

Place branding as has been abovementioned analyzed, is mainly a contemporary strategy which aims to resynthesize collective identities that have been influenced from changes that have taken in the end of the 20th century and still continue to exist in the 21st century.

Its aim is not just the attraction of visitors on a seasonal basis for consumption of selective tourist products or specific elements of the place identity. The aim is that the exisitng and potential visitors and the public opinion to connect the place with its cultural heritage and its whole identity, to develop in that way, the recognizable identity which defines and differentiates it from others. We need to take into consideration that competitiveness of whole countries, entities, such as regions and cities exists and competition in tourism has intensified (Papp and Raffay, 2011). Being competitive for a tourism destination is associated with the tourism expenditure, to increasingly attract visitors, to satisfy and provide them with memorable experiences; at the same time, residents need to be happy and the natural capital of the destination should be preserved (Ritchie and Crough in Papp and Raffay, 2011: 23).

Culture has a significant role to play during the procedure of enrichment of the image of a region irrespective of its spatial and administrative size, as a unique characteristic. This takes place because via culture a more complete understanding of values that this place serves takes place from the tourists. As a result, culture consists of a dynamic element within the framework of branding strategy; in addition, the sense of quality that is associated with culture is not related to the market needs and the return of investment as is the case with businesses (Belch and Belch, 2009). All the people involved for the culture's production, creators and target groups ask to be participants to a true experience (Anholt, 2007: 97-99). Therefore, the cultural perspective of the image of a place is unique and authentic and is associated with its past and its present (Bitsani, 2004: 93). As has been mentioned in Chapter 6, the cultural heritage of great wealth can be a key factor to enhance the brand image of a place (Alonso and Bea, 2012).

The private sector may contribute a lot to the contemporary image of a place but also volunteers and associations in order to create co-operations and promote the region. Rather than putting all the effort on the image management, public relations may help with the relationship building with national and international media but also with the creation of social media and the prevention of dealing with negative publicity -in case negative associations have been made for a place-. All the cultural and social entities of a region need to be incorporated within the framework of the implementation of policies of place and destination branding and place marketing; to this end, relationship building may contribute the most (Szondi, 2010).

By creating networks among the agents involved emotional attachment and relationship maintenance is enhanced among the interested parties involved, residents, to name but a few. Such relations need to be symbiotic; collaboration and cooperation to bring about common good for the community and enhance residents' own interests, -both as people living in a region and as businessmen who develop economic activity in the area. Nevertheless, networks are not fully implemented in order to contribute to the branding of places and at times, they are not existent at all. Authors call for research on the role of networkrs and the cooperation among the private and local sector where they could advertise a region and its distinct characteristics in the virtual environment; communities, places, regions can be branded online as well (Kavoura and Katsoni, 2013; Lee, Lee, Taylor and Lee, 2011). This is the focus of the next Chapter.

Chapter 8

THE USE OF NEW TECHNOLOGIES FOR THE CREATION OF AN E- PLACE BRAND AND E-PLACE MARKETING

In a competitive world and in an era of technological, economic and social developments, within the framework of crisis and recession, in order for geographic but also organizational entities to safeguard their sustainability, to raise the numbers of visitors and to have economic viability, they need to adjust to the new environment promoting the resources they have while implementing their policies in order to communicate their messages to the related target groups.

Places, either centrally located or isolated, may promote themselves based their strategies on new technologies and social media. Peripheries' work may be enhanced ands reinforced since European peripheral strategy promotes measures and directives in order to empower peripheral and local development; thus, local communities and their representatives at administrative and political level have a role to play. The place identity and its distinct characteristics can be asserted based on local attitudes (Ooi, 2004).

EU regional policy although aiming to empower regions, has not taken into consideration the experience of these regions in order to realize which their needs are (Petrakos, 2012: 27). Integration is nevertheless, not a a space neutral process, as it is characterized by space selectivity and the environment is unfavorable for lagging-behind regions in the EU. Territorial approaches should be more flexible and more adaptive to local and regional needs (Petrakos, 2012: 27). The implementation of new technologies has been used from countries in an effort to help countries position themselves in the world to raise their competitiveness, to creation job opportunities, to be innovative, to cooperate between countries and places (El Sayed and Westrup, 2003).

Research has paid attention to the fact that there is need to respond to the new opportunities opened by technological development and effort should be put into producing lively and imaginative websites which are emerging as branding tools in their own right; websites provide an innovative way recently employed to develop experiences and their communication to tourists to participate to a place (Carlsen, Liburd, Edwards and Forde, 2008: 70-72; Lin, Pearson and Cai, 2011: 33) while electronic branding has yet to be adequately conceptualized (Dunn and Hogg, 2010; Hjalager, 2010; Lee, Lee, Taylor and Lee, 2011).

The basic characteristics of the technologies of internet are associated with a flexible management of data, potential access to all for the design of the network but also for its use, promotion of culture and cooperation; the adoption of communication and information technologies could positively contribute to the local development (Borges-Tiago et al., 2007).

In addition, internet penetration in different countries is significant in order for advertisers and marketers to be able to know if and to what degree they may use the internet, since there are differentiations to the use of internet from country to country (Gong, Li and Stump, 2007).

Places and their authorities are not always responsive to the use of new technologies (see for example, the limited use of new technologies employed in Arcadia, Greece in order to promote the religious tourism of the region, Kavoura and Katsoni, 2013).

The provision of promotional material can be significant for a destination and the enhancement of its place identity. Nevertheless, this is not always the case. Research for example, in mountainous regions illustrated that tourism management may concentrate on the ways of attracting the visitors and mainly on accessibility, tourism infrastructure, preservation of natural beauty contrary to the hypothesis made that informative advertising promotional material locally, nationally and internationally is a necessity (Bitsani and Kavoura, 2013).

It should also be taken into consideration that for many places which employ new technologies in order to promote their distinct characteristics and attract visitors, investments, migrants, new technologies are not panacea. Advertising via media channels is not communication for its own sake; it has a capacity to communicate cultural meaning and resonate ideological tenets with consumers (Kilamby, et al., 2013: 48). The consumer creation of mental pictures may lead to behavioral responses and this may take place if the message incorporates multiple sensory inputs as vivid stimuli according to

Stern, Zinkhan and Holbrook (2002: 23) -although they did not initially refer to places.

Thus, new technologies and the way the communication message is constructed in order to employ the internet as a tool, may lead to the creation of a virtual community -a group of people who may or may not meet one another face-to face and who exchange words and ideas through the mediation of computer bulletin boards and networks (Garrigos-Simon et al., 2012: 1881)- ICTs can be the communication tools which promote the distinct characteristics of such a community. Internet allows the communication on one-to-one basis, one-to-all-to-one basis and one-to-all basis (Siomkos and Tsiamis, 2004: 206). In addition, this participation, is the result of the social need that the person has to communicate and interact with others belonging in a community which can take place on the internet.

An example with the case study of Carinthia, Austria (Kavoura and Bitsani, 2013) brings forth the necessity of Internet use in the era of crisis for the promotion of a region and its revitalization but also the necessity of network creation among all the people involved towards the procedure of development, promotion and communication of a region or a place as a destination as the connecting node which will orient and orchestrate all the powers and synergies while decisions will be under its responsibility (Kavoura and Bitsani, 2013).

The general themes that we searched in the data of all the websites of rural Carinthia were associated with the tangible elements in the creation of a brand; Kavoura and Bitsani (2013) defined that the tangible elements can be associated with natural, cultural, gastronomical resources as the distinct characteristics of the region or a place. The presence of intangible elements were also examined and the promotion of emotion may lead to argue for an e-brand of a region and in the abovementioned case of a rural region; emotion is the element that adds to the promotion of e- branding of rural tourism. This is another way for the conceptualization of e-branding with all the senses to participate, forming knowledge structures that the tourist/visitor is familiar with for the promotion of subjective emotional values (Kavoura and Bitsani, 2013). These functional attributes of place branding together with tangible attributes, create the brand image for places in combination with intangible and symbolic attributes and values are incorporated (Campelo et al., 2011: 4).

Destination marketing may gather information from word of mouth, mass media, travel agents, tour operators and personal experiences (Balakrishnan et al., 2011: 5). Tourists acquire knowledge from their own experiences, those of others and visual and sensory stimuli, all of which educate them about destination image; destination image is formed from communication inputs throughout one's lifetime and tourists retain messages that are relevant to them (Molina and Esteban, 2006: 1039).

Policy makers and marketers should take into consideration that visitors are positive to find out information about places employing new technologies (Yuksel et al., 2010: 274; Prayag and Ryan, 2012: 342; Katsoni, 2011).

Chapter 9

THE NEW ROLE OF THE PUBLIC SECTOR: NEGOTIATING THE CONCEPT OF THE PUBLIC INTEREST TO THE NEW CONDITIONS AS A BASIC POLE OF A STRATEGIC PLAN FOR PLACE BRANDING-PLACE MARKETING

Networks, including networks of social partners, entrepreneural partners, agents of local economy, citizens of a place, is necessary; they need to participate and cooperate in order to design sustainable activities for an area but they may be also adjusted and used for other areas. Networks need to take into account the Information and Communication Technologies in order to avoid digital isolation.

The contribution of a co-ordinator, an advisor, will guarantee the equal participation of all and the legitimacy of choices and policies towards the common interest of all. The common interest is the public interest. Literature has shown that the co-ordinator can be from another country or a private sector stakeholder who has experience in related issues of cooperation among different agents (Jones in McGehee et al., 2010: 489).

The necessity of aiming of all the policy plans and activities in a place irrespective of its spatial size and irrespective of the legal entity of this agent, has mainly been focused on culture at local level, where the public interest's significance was found (Bitsani, 2004), since "a cultural activity is defined as the organized communication of consumers -users of cultural products, their use and thus, their elevation. Such communication takes the form of a social event, in other words, it could be included to the social phenomena, while it is also necessary and beneficial to the cultural creator but also for the society (Bitsani, 2004: 32-33).

Public interest refers to the society which creates a state, to a population which may be consisted of different ethnicities. Public interest needs to include and not be indifferent for those who do not have the citizenship of the specific state. It is only in that way, community may succesfully operate. Unfortunately, this is not the case for all countries. Taking Greece as an example, which is located in a territory where disputes at its borders take place due to its geopolitical position -in that it connects Europe with Asia- it experienced and continues to experience migrations since the mid 1990s; "to date no law for immigration has been established in Greece" (Kavoura, 2013: 71) creating a xenophobic and ethnocentric approach towards people from other countries who live in Greece. This perspective at times, does not allow the country to realize the multicultural world in which its people live. Due to globalization conditions which have taken the power over states, public interest may refer to small local communities.

Public interest is associated with the benefit of the whole society and this is where the local authorities have a role to play in order to safeguard the "public or social interest" of every region. Local authorities may encourage initiatives, co-ordinate whatever can be prodcutive with the citizen's participation, safeguarding the necessary resources (Bitsani, 2004: 269). Specifically, the local authorities are responsible each time to connect to a component all the interests of society at a particular time and place and on that basis to design strategies at local and regional level in the direction of sustainable holistic development.

A branding and marketing strategy should take into consideration the public interest, the cooperation, the participation of local authorities and entities will be the new pole of attraction and the co-ordinators of the strategic mix of place destination branding and place marketing towards the necessity of implementation of a holistic strategy and development, which will continuously elevate the tourist product and the place via a place brand based on place identity and the human will be before the markets.

The implementation of a connecting strategy for the marketing of a region will have a holistic approach and will continuously seek for the elevation of the product on offer and the place. The human and his/her needs will be in priority based on criteria that safeguard social benefit. It will evaluate the possibilities for the protection and sustainable development of tourist resources (natural, social, cultural) of these areas as tourist destinations. All the small and big powers of a place, social and productive are called to play a significant role. Legislation may allow for more cooperation to be initiated and take place. In regard to the Greek case for example, Public Private Partnerships (PPPs) allow for the cooperation of the public and private sector and constitute an important reform employing the existing framework of the public sector.

Within this framework, every place, every region, is called to define specific criteria of public interest that will allow everyone to benefit under a healthy competition.

Chapter 10

PROPOSITION FOR THE FUTURE: A MODEL OF SYSTEMIC APPROACH OF THE STRATEGIC DESIGN OF PLACE MARKETING AND PLACE BRANDING

The analysis of the previous chapters illustrated that in contemporary conditions, place identity has a significant role to play, is in the first line and is reinforced from national identity. The strategic plans for the promotion of a place are based on national and place identity implemented from key players.

The key players to a marketing plan for the promotion of a place and its branding are the private sector, the public sector, the human resources -internal and external-, the implementation of new technologies, the media and the internet as communication tools, the natural capital of each place, the social capital of the place and its cultural capital. This results in a place branding that is chosen by people. The connecting element of the successful place branding and place marketing can be the social public interest.

The key players to a marketing plan for the promotion of a place and its branding are the private sector, the public sector, the human resources -internal and external-, the implementation of new technologies, the media and the internet as communication tools, the natural capital of each place, the social capital of the place and its cultural capital. This results into a place branding that is chosen by people. The connecting element of the successful place branding and place marketing can be the public social interest.

The public interest is the basic principal of the whole strategy and a pole of attraction for such implementation in a specific time and place; local authorities which are close to the citizen and his/her most direct representatives need to operate keeping in mind the common interest, whether this is related to residents of a place but also to the visitors. Exclusions cannot take place; we live in a multicultural world and there are many examples where ethnocentrism prevails (Tomaras and Frigkas, 2008). The social public interest connects, unites and motivates all the powers of the public and private interest reinforced by the imagiend community advanced by public and private sector synergies and networks.

Local authorities of a place are close to citizens and represent local communities, take the role of the coordinator of the whole strategy having as the axis the public social interest. A basic element of place marketing and a necessary prerequisite is the creation of a brand based on the identity of the place. Networking of all those involved towards a holistic approach of sustainable development of a region should guarantee that all the points of view are heard and more importantly, that all the agents involved become participants of the branding of the region.

The creation of synergies can offer the promotion of a consistent whole for the potential tourist who may associate the region that adopts similar ways of promotion as a sacred place, a place which is different, has an order, everything is under control and organized. Synergies between teams can offer effective results for the promotion of an area and co-ordination of agencies' activities (Carlsen, Liburd, Edwards and Forde, 2008: 70-72; Nylander and Hall, 2005: 24) is effective enough. The result is that each part of the synergy provides knowledge and combines capacities filling in the parts of the team.

Then, strategic policies take into consideration how best to match the interests of people (as potential target groups, existing visitors, stakeholders, investors, other governments etc) with the distinct characteristics of a place. In that way, the effort will be made to sentimental bonds with a place that will function on a real or virtual basis, having common elements to share among them.

New technologies will contribute to the implementation of the strategic policies. Nevertheless, advertising as a message intended at a specific audience from a specific person, state, stakeholder who promotes this message, should have an 'effective community of minds' in order for the message to be received, taking into consideration the prior knowledge of the target group (Kilamby et al. 2013:49). The results indicate that the concept of the imagined community can be associated with tourism (Kavoura and Katsoni, 2013); although from a different scientific approach (Kavoura and Stavrianea, under review) argue that the concept of the imagined community can be used as an interpretative tool in order to better understand the connection a tourist can develop with a place (Kavoura and Stavrianea, under review). It is thus, worthwhile to employ contemporary marketing constructs in order to be able to operationalize and measure the concept of the imagined community in relation to them.

In that way, we argue an 'imagined community' is created among and between different groups, internal and external, which allows the connection to take place and be strong if there is familiarity and sentimental bonding between people and a place creating and enhancing the branding of the place. On the contrary, it may not take place if there is not so much bonding attached to a place. The more a place understands the feelings of the visitors, the more the relation can be expanded and it will be reciprocal since visitors will also contribute to the continuous enhancement of the place identity elements taking into consideration the socio-political and economic environment. To these, we should have in mind the public interest.

An example can make the case clearer in regard to the visitors, the role of public authorities and the public social interest is the following: Greece has many sites of religious significance for the Orthodox populations all over the world. The Greek state realizing such a potential for branding Greece as a religious destination -employing the distinct elements of the nation's or different places' identity- may make easier the procedures for visitors requiring visa in order to visit Greece (such as Russians who are religiously oriented to Greece because of the common Orthodox religion). Visitors can be segmented based on their preferences which can be associated with the capital of the specific place (eg. religious heritage tourism, see Kavoura, 2013: 81). Another aspect of the imagined community as a connecting element and point of visitor attraction is the presentation of Greece as the cornerstone of the Western civilization; thus, elements of place identity which are also elements of the national identity eg. the Acropolis or antiquity sites can bring together people attached to the classical ideals. Then, an attempt can be made to relate a brand community which is "a specialized, non-geographically bound community, based on a structured set of social relationships among admirers of a brand (Muniz and O' Guinn in Kilamby et al., 2013: 46) with Anderson's (1991) imagined community as Kavoura and Stavrianea (under review) argue for the connection of the imagined community with place identity.

The main parameters presented and discussed above are presented graphically in a model as a figure next (Figure 1). All the elements of the abovementioned Figure (Figure 1) are in continuous interrelation one with the other. Synergies need to be created among the private and public sector so that strategic policies are initiated and implemented with the use of new technologies taking into consideration the social public interest. For this to be realized, the design and the construction of a strategic marketing plan is needed in order for place branding to be implemented. In regard to the content of the strategic policies, they are informed by elements of the national and place identity with the aim of transforming them into place branding employing tangible and intangible resources. Based on that, e-branding and e-marketing can be the next step in places' advertising and promotion in the 21st century where the use of information and communication technologies is in the first line of use. The application of total quality management as a management tool in the design and implementation of place brand and place marketing consists, according to our point of view, the ideal method for achieving the best possible results. Total quality management will contribute to focus on the performance and effectiveness bringing together the public and the private sector. Marketing has reached another era (Thlikidou-Stogianni, 2003). The implementation of the Total Quality Management in the design and management of the place marketing plan consists of the next part of our research since it is an open field of research.

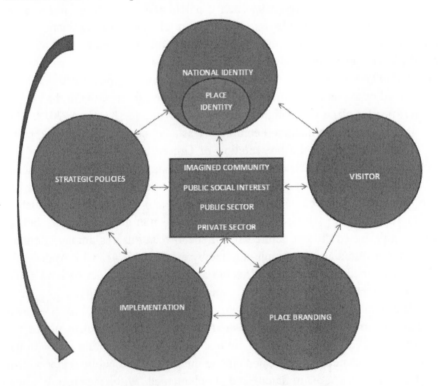

Figure 1. A Proposed Model of Place Marketing and Place Branding

REFERENCES

Ampuero, O. & Vila, N. (2006). Consumer perceptions of product packaging. *Journal of Consumer Research*, 23(2), 100-112.

Alonso, I. & Bea, E. (2012). A tentative model to measure city brands on the Internet. *Place Branding and Public Diplomacy*, 8(4), 311–328.

Anderson, B. (1991). Imagined Communities, (2nd ed). London: Verso.

Andersson, M. & Ekman, P. (2009). Ambassador networks and place branding. *Journal of Place Management and Development*, 2 (1), 41-51.

Anholt, S. (2005). Editorial: Some important distinctions in place branding. *Place Branding and Public Diplomacy*, 1(2), 116-121.

Anholt, S. (2007). Competitive Identity. *The New Brand Management for Nations, Cities and Regions*. Basingstoke, UK: Palgrave Macmillan.

Balakrishnan, M., Nekhili, R. & Lewis, C. (2011). Destination Brand Components. *International Journal of Culture, Tourism and Hospitality Research,* 5(1), 4-25.

Belch, E & Belch, M. (2009). *Advertising and Promotion* (8th ed.). USA: The McGraw- Hill.

Bellou, F. (2013). *American Leadership Image and the Yugoslav Crisis.* Germany: Saarbrucken.

Bennett, R. & Rundle Thiele, S. (2004). Customer Satisfaction Should not be the only Goal. *Journal of Services Marketing*, 16(7), 514-523.

Bitsani, E. (2004). Culture Management and Regional Development. *Culture Policy Planning and Cultural Product Planning.* Athens: Dionicos, (in Greek).

Bitsani, E. (2006). *Human Resources Management* (in Greek). Athens: Dionikos.

Bitsani, E. & Kavoura, A. (2010). Application of the rural tour methodology for advertising and promoting rural areas in Eastern Europe. In Karasavvogolou (Ed), *The Economies of the Balkan and Eastern Europe Countries in the Changed World* (pp. 306-322), Cambridge: Cambridge Publishing.

Bitsani, E. & Kavoura, A. (2011). Organizational networks, migration, and intercultural relations in Trieste, Italy. *International Journal of Culture, Tourism and Hospitality Research*, 5(1), 26-37.

Bitsani, E. & Kavoura, A. (2012). Connecting Enological and gastronomical tourisms at the Wine Roads, Veneto, Italy for the promotion and development of agrotourism. *Journal of Vacation Marketing*, 18(4), 301-312.

Bitsani, E. & Kavoura, A. (2014). *Host Perceptions of RURAL TOUR Marketing to Sustainable Tourism in Central Eastern Europe. The Case Study of Istria, Croatia.* 2nd International Conference on Strategic Innovative Marketing, 13-17 September Prague, ELSEVIER (in press).

Bitsani, E. & Kavoura, A. (2013). Accessibility versus advertising for mountain tourism: the case of Nafpaktia, Greece. *Tourismos*, 8(1) (in press).

Borges-Tiago. M. T., Couto, J., dos Santos Natário, M. & Braga, A. (2007). The Adoption of Communication and Information Technologies and the Local Development. *Journal of Business Economics and Management*, 8(2), 111-117.

Brakus, J., Schmitt, B. & Zarantonello, L. (2009). Brand Experience: What is it? How is it Measured? Does it affect loyalty? *Journal of Marketing*, 73(1), 52-68.

Braun, E., Kavaratzis, M. & Zenker, S. (2010). My City-My Brand: The Role of Residents in Place Branding, 50th *European Regional Science Association Congress*, 19-23 August, Sweden.

Breman, B., Vihinen, H., Tapio-Bistrom, M.-L. & Pinto Correia, M. T. (2010). Meeting the Challenge of Marginalization Processes at the Periphery of Europe. *Public Administration*, 88, 364–380.

Buhalis, D. (2000). Marketing the competitive destination of the futrure. *Tourism Management*, 21(1), 97-116.

Calvert, P. (1991) Using Documentary Sources. in G. Allan, & C. Skinner (Eds.) *Handbook for Research Students in the Social Sciences*, (pp. 117-127), London: Falmer.

Campelo, A., Aitken, R., & Gnoth, J. (2011). Visual Rhetoric and Ethics in Marketing of Destinations. *Journal of Travel Research*, 50(1), 3-14.

Cano, L. & Mysyk, A. (2004). Cultural tourism, the State and Day of the Dead. *In Annals of Tourism Research*, 31(4), 879-898.

Carlisle, S. (1998). Lalibela (Ethiopia), Visitor Management Case Studies for World Heritage Sites, in M. Shackley (Ed), *Visitor Management Case Studies for World Heritage Sites,* (pp. 139-159), Oxford: Butterworth-Heinemann.

Carlsen, J., Liburd, J., Edwards, D. & Forde, P. (2008). *Innovation for Sustainable Tourism, International Case Studies.* Denmark: Best EN-University of Southern Denmark.

Cassel, S. (2008). Trying to be attractive: Image building and identity formation in small industrial municipalities in Sweden. *Place Branding and Public Diplomacy*, 4(2), 102–114.

Citta del Vino (2011). Osservatorio sul Turismo del Vino, IX Rapporto annuale, Sensis, Servizi: Associazone Nazionale. (http://www.terredelvino.net/sites/default/files/IX%20RAPPORTO%20FINALE%20O K_0.pdf)

Christou, E. (2004). The impact of trust on brand loyalty: evidence from the hospitality industry. *Tourist Scientific Review*, 1(1), 63-74.

Daugstad, K. (2008). Negotiating Landscape in Rural Tourism, *Annals of Tourism Research*, 35(2), 402-426.

Dinnie, K. (2008). *Nation Branding. Concepts, Issues, Practice.* Oxford: Butterworth-Heinemann.

Dodd, T. (1999). Attracting Repeat Customers to Wineries. *International Journal of Wine Marketing*, 11(2), 18-28.

Dunn, D. & Hogg, D. (2010). Marketing the Uniqueness of Small Towns. Western Rural Development Center 1995. Available at: http://www.msue.edu/msue/imp/modtd/33529767.html (accessed 4 May 2013).

Durie, A., Yeoman, I. & McMahon-Beattie, U. (2006). How the history of Scotland creates a sense of place. *Place Branding and Public Diplomacy*, 2(1), 43–52.

El Sayed, H. & Westrup, C. (2003). Egypt and ICTs. How ICTs bring national initiatives, global organizations and local companies together. *Information Technology and People*, 16(1), 76-92.

Europe Innova (2008). *Cluster policy in Europe A brief summary of cluster policies in 31 European countries.* Europe Innova Cluster Mapping Project: Oxford Research.

European Commission (1999). *Towards quality rural tourism. Integrated Quality Management (IQM) of rural tourist destinations.* Brussels, Enterprise Directorate–General Tourism Unit.

European Committee (2000). Committee's Announcement to the member states on the 14th of April 2000 for the determination of the general directions for European Initiative in regard to rural development (Leader+), *Official Newspaper of the European Commmunities.*

Feilden, M. B. & Jokilehto, J. (1993). *Management Guidelines for World Cultural Heritage Sites.* Roma: ICCROM.

Fine, H. S. (1981). *The Marketing of Ideas and Social Issues* New York: Praeger.

Fopp, M. A. (1997). Organisation Structure. In M.Fopp (Ed.) *Managing Museums and Galleries* (pp. 135-147), London: Roultedge.

Forster, N. (1994). The Analysis of Company Documentation.. In C. Cassell & G. Symon (Eds.) *Qualitative Methods in Organizational Research: A Practical Guide* (pp. 147-166), London: Sage.

Freeman, B. & Nhung Nguyen, T. (2012). Seeing Singapore: Portrayal of the city-state in global print media. *Place Branding and Public Diplomacy*, 8(2), 158–169.

Garrigos-Simon, J., Alcamı´, L. & Ribera, B. (2012). Social networks and Web 3.0: their impact on the management and marketing of organizations. *Management Decision*, 50(10), 1880-1890.

Gellner, E. (1983*). Nations and Nationalism* Oxford: Basil, Blackwell.

Gilmore, F. (2002). A country-can it be repositioned? Spain-the success story of a country branding. *The Journal of Brand Management*, 9(4-5), 281-293.

Global Financial Stability Report (2011). *Grappling with Crisis Legacies*, IMF: Washington DC.

Gong, W., Li, Z. & Stump, R. (2007). Global internet use and access: cultural considerations. *Asia Pacific Journal of Marketing and Logistics*, 19(1), 57-74.

Govers, R. (2005). *Virtual Tourism Destination Image. Glocal identities constructed, perceived and experiences*, Erasmus Research Institute of Management: Netherlands.

Govers, R. & Go, F. (2005). Projected Destination Image Online: Website Content Analysis of Pictures and Text. *Information Technology & Tourism*, 7(1), 73-89.

Gow, J. & Bellou, F. (2003). Image and intervention, leadership and legitimacy: The dynamics of Euro-Atlantic engagement with challenges to international peace and security. *Civil Wars*, 6(1), 33-52.

Hall, M. C. & Jenkins, J. M. (1995). *Tourism and Public Policy*. London & New York: Routledge.

Hall, M. C. & McArthur, S. (1993). The Marketing of Heritage. In M. Hall. And S. McArthur (Eds.) *Heritage Management in New Zealand and Australia: Visitor Management, Interpretation and Marketing* (pp. 40-47), Auckland, NZ, Oxford University Press.

Hankinson, G. (2004). Relational network brands: Towards a conceptual model of place brands. *Journal of Vacation Marketing*, 10(2), 109-121.

Hanna, S. & Rowley, J. (2008). An analysis of terminology use in place branding. *Place Branding and Public Diplomacy*, 4(1), 61-75.

Haralambopoulos, N. & Pizam, A. (1996). Perceived impacts of tourism: the case of Samos. *Annals of Tourism Research*, 23(3), 503-526.

Hartley, F. J. (1994). Case Studies in Organizational Research. In C. Cassell & G. Symon (Eds.) *Qualitative Methods in Organizational Research: A Practical Guide* (pp. 208-229), London: Sage.

Herrmann, J. (1989). World Archaeology- the world's cultural heritage. In H. Cleere (Ed.) *Archaeological heritage management in the modern world* (pp. 30-37), London: Unwin, Hyman (translated by Katherine Judelson).

Hidalgo, C. & Hernández, B. (2001). Place Attachment: Conceptual and Empirical Questions. *Journal of Environmental Psychology*, 21(3), 273-281.

Hjalager, A. (2010). A review of innovation research in tourism. *Tourism Management* 31(1), 1-12. Available at: http://www.hotelara.com/travel/austria/accommodation/carinthia.html (accessed 8 January 2013).

Hjortegaard Hansen, R. (2010). The narrative nature of place branding, *Place Branding and Public Diplomacy*, 6(4), 268–279.

http://www.conservation.org/xp/CIWEB/programs/ecotourism/ecotourism.xml (accessed 8.06.2013).

http://www.istheory.yorku.ca/socialnetworktheory.htm (accessed 8.06.2013).

Hummon, D. (1986). City Mouse, Country Mouse: The Persistence of Community Identity. *Qualitative Sociology*, 9(1), 3-25.

Hwang J, McMillan, S. & Lee, G. (2003). Corporate Web Sites as Advertising: An Analysis of Function, Audience and Message Strategy. *Journal of Interactive Advertising* 3(2). Available at: http://www.jiad.org (accessed 10 March 2013).

Izzo, P. (2012). Why Did Unemployment Rate Increase? Real Times Economics http://blogs.wsj.com/economics/2012/08/03/why-did-unemploment-rate-increase/ 12.7.2013

Jackson, J. (1984). *Discovering the vernacular Landsc*ape. New Haven: Yale University Press.

Kapferer, J. N. (2013). *Brand Management, Contemporary Approaches* (Translation Rigopoulou, I.) (1st ed.), Athens: Rosili.

Karvelyte, K. & Chiu, J.C. (2011). Planning process of city brands: A case study of Taipei. City. *Place Branding and Public Diplomacy*, 7(4), 257-270.

Katsoni, V. (2011). The Role of ICTs in Regional Tourist Development. *Regional Science Inquiry Journal*, 3(2), 95-113.

Kavaratzis, M. & Ashworth, G. (2008). Place Marketing: how did we get here and where are we going? *Journal of Place Management and Development*, 1(2), 150-165.

Kavoura, A. (2001). *State policy for the presentation of Greek National Heritage: the case of the Cultural World Heritage Sites*. Phd Thesis. University of Stirling, Stirling, UK [http://www.is.stir.ac.uk/research/theses/digitisation.php].

Kavoura, A. (2005). Approaching 'Cultural Assets' from an Economic Perspective. *Review of Economic Sciences*, 7(1), 55-78.

Kavoura, A. (2006). Application of Marketing Communications in the Promotion of English language teaching books. How does it work for British and Greek publishing houses? Scientific Research Review Επιστημονική Επετηρίδα Εφαρμοσμένης Έρευνας (in Greek), XI(2), 181-203.

Kavoura, A. (2007). Advertising of National Identity and Tourism Bureaucracy. *Current Issues in Tourism*, 10(3), 399-414.

Kavoura, A. (2013). Politics of Heritage Promotion: Branding the Identity of the Greek State. *Tourism, Culture and Communication*, 12(2/3), 69-83.

Kavoura, A. (2014). A Conceptual Communication Model for Nation Branding in the Greek Framework. Implications for Strategic Advertising Policy. 2nd International Conference on Strategic Innovative Marketing, 13-17 September Prague, ELSEVIER (in press).

Kavoura, A. & Bitsani, E. (2013). E-branding of Rural Tourism in Carinthia, Austria. *Tourism*, 61(3).

Kavoura, A. & Bitsani, E. (2014). Methodological Considerations for Qualitative Communication Research. 2nd International Conference on Strategic Innovative Marketing, 13-17 September Prague, ELSEVIER (in press).

Kavoura, A. & Katsoni, V. (2013). Advertising a religious 'imagined community' and consumer tourism behavior: the case of branding a prefecture at a local level, Arcadia, Greece, *Advertising: Types of Methods, Perceptions and Impact on Consumer Behavior*. USA: Nova Publishers (in press).

Kavoura, A. & Stavrianea, K. (under review) Relating the 'imagined community' with brand experiences and destination branding: a proposed model for brand loyalty. *Journal of Travel and Tourism Marketing*.

Kemp, E., Childers, C. & Williams, K. (2012). A tale for a musical city: Fostering self-brand connection among residents of Austin, Texas. *Place Branding and Public Diplomacy*, 8(2), 147–157.

Kerrigan, F., Shivanandan, J. & Hede, A-M (2012). Nation Branding. A Critical Appraisal of Incredible India. *Journal of Macromarketing*, 32(3), 319-327.

Kilamby, A., Laroche, M. & Richard, M-O. (2013). Constitutive Marketing. Towards understanding brand community formation. *International Journal of Advertising*, 32(1), 45-64.

Kim, P. (1990). A perspective on brands. *Journal of Consumer Marketing*, 7(4), 63-67.

Kirby, G. V. (1993). Landscape, Heritage and Identity Stories from the West Coast. In *Heritage Management in New Zealand and Australia: Visitor Management, Interpretation and Marketing* (pp. 119-129), Auckland, NZ: Oxford University Press.

Kiriakidis, S. (2008). Application of the theory of planned behaviour to recidivism: the role of personal norm in predicting behavioural intentions of re-offending. *Journal of Applied Social Psychology*, 38(9), 2210-2221.

Konečnik, M. (2004). Evaluating Slovenia's image as a tourism destination: A self-analysis process towards building a destination brand. *Brand Management*, 11(4), 307-316.

Konečnik, M. & Go, F. (2008). Tourism Destination brand identity: The case of Slovenia, *Brand Management*, 15(3), 177-189.

Kotler, P., Armstrong, G., Saunders, J. & Wong V. (2001). *Principles of Marketing* (3rd European ed.). FT/Prentice Hall Europe.

Kotler, P. & Keller, K. (2012). *Marketing Management* (14th ed.). Boston: Pearson.

Kotler, P., Haider, D. H. & Rein, I. (1993). *Marketing Places: Attracting Investment, Industry, and Tourism to Cities, States, and Nations*. New York: Free Press.

Koutouzis, M. (1999). *General Principles of Management*. Patra: Hellenic Open University.

Kristiansen, K. (1989). Perspectives on the archaeological heritage: history and future. In H. Cleere (Ed.) *Archaeological heritage management in the modern world,* (pp. 23-29), London: Unwin, Hyman.

Kuscer, K. (2013). Determining Factors of mountain destination innovativeness. *Journal of Vacation Marketing*, 19(1), 41-54.

Kyle, G., Bricker, K., Graefe, A. & Wickham, T. (2004). An examination of recreationists' relationships with activities and settings. *Leisure Sciences*, 26(2), 123-142.

Lee, H.J., Lee, D. H., Taylor, C.R. & Lee, J.H. (2011). Do online brand communities help build and maintain relationships with consumers? A network theory approach. *Journal of Brand Management*, 19(3), 213-227.

Lichrou, M., O'Malley, L. & Patterson, M. (2010). Narratives of a tourism destination: Local particularities and their implications for place marketing and branding. *Place Branding and Public Diplomacy*, 6(2), 134–144.

Lin Y, Pearson, T. & Cai, L. (2011). Food as a Form of Destination Identity: A Tourism Destination Brand Perspective. *Tourism and Hospitality Research,* 11(1), 30-48.

Lowenthal, D. (1994). Identity, Heritage, and History. In R. J. Gillis (Ed.) Commemorations, *The Politics of National Identity* (pp. 41-57), Princeton, NJ: Princeton University Press.

Lundqvist, A., Liljander, V., Gummerus, J. & van Riel, A. (2013). The impact of storytelling on the consumer brand experience: The case of a firm-originated story. *Journal of Brand Management*, 20(4), 283–297.

Lytras, P. (2005). Investigation of Development of alternative Forms of Tourism in the islands of Greece through related education. *Management and Economy*, 3(2), 255-258 (in Greek).

MacDonald, R. & Jolliffe, L. (2003). Cultural rural tourism: Evidence from Canada. *Annals of Tourism Research*, 30(2), 307-322.

Marzano, G. & Scott, N. (2009). Power in destination Branding. *Annals of Tourism Research,* 36(2), 247-267.

Marzo-Navarro, M. & Pedraja-Iglesias, M. (2009). Wine tourism development from the perspective of the potential tourist in Spain. *International Journal of Contemporary Hospitality Management*, 21(7), 816-835.

Masser, I., Sviden, O. & Wegener, M. (1992). *The Geography of Europe's Future*. London and New York, Belhaven Press.

Maxwell, J. (1996). *Qualitative Research Design: An Interactive Approach.* London: Sage.

Maykut, P. & Morehouse, R. (1994). *Beginning Qualitative Research. A Philosophic and Practical Guide.* London: The Falmer Press.

McGehee, N., Lee, S., Bannon, T. & Perdue, R. (2010). Tourism-related Social Capital and its Relationship with Other Forms of Capital: An Exploratory Study. *Journal of Travel Research*, 49(4), 486-500.

Meenagham, T. (1995). The role of Advertising in Brand Image Development. *Journal of Product and Brand Management*, 4(4), 23-34.

Ministero Dello Sviluppo Economico (2011). http://italianmade.com/wine-details/bardolino-superiore-5-106.html.

Mitsche, N., Vogt, F., Knox, D, Cooper, I. Lombardi, P. & Ciaffi, D. (2013). Intangibles: enhancing access to cities' cultural heritage through interpretation. International Journal of Culture. *Tourism and Hospitality Research,* 7(1), 68-77.

Mlozi, S., Pesamaa, O., Haahti, A. & Salunke, S. (2013). Determinants of place identity and dependence: the Case of International Tourists in Tanzania. *Tourism, Culture and Communication*, 12(2/3), 97-114.

Molina, A., & Esteban, Á. (2006). Tourism Brochures, Usefulness and Image. *Annals of Tourism Research*, 33(4), 1036-1056.

Morgan, N. & Pritchard, A. (2002). Contextualising destination branding. In N. Morgan, A. Pritchard and R. Pride (Eds.) *Destination Branding: Creating the unique destination proposition* (pp. 11-41), Oxford: Butterworth-Heinemann.

Northover, J. (2010). A brand for Belfast: How can branding a city influence change? *Place Branding and Public Diplomacy*, 6(2), 104-111.

Nuryanti, W. (1996). Heritage and Postmodern Tourism. *Annals of Tourism Research*, 23(2), 249-260.

Nylander, M. & Hall, D. (2005). Rural Tourism Policy. European Perspectives. In D. Hall, I. Kirkpatrick and M. Mitchell (Eds.) *Rural*

Tourism and Sustainable Business (pp. 17-40), USA: Channel View Publications.

O' Boyle, N. (2011). *New Vocabularies, Old Ideas* (Reimagining Ireland). Bern: Peter Lang.

O' Donohoe, S. (2011). New Vocabularies, Old Ideas: Culture, Irishness and the Advertising Industry-Neil O'Boyle. *International Journal of Advertising*, 30(3), 538-540.

Olins, W. (2002). Branding the nation – the historical context. *Journal of Brand Management*, 9(4/5), 241-248.

Ooi, C.S. (2004). Poetics and Politics of Destination Branding: Denmark. *Scandinavian Journal of Hospitality and Tourism*, 4(2), 107-128.

Ooi, C.S. (2011). Branding and the accreditation approach: Singapore. In N. Morgan, A. Pritchard and R. Pride (3rd Eds.) *Destination Brands. Managing Place Reputation* (pp. 185-196), Oxford: Elsevier Ltd.

Ooi, C.S. & Pedersen, S. (2010). City branding and film festivals: Re-evaluating stakeholder's relations. *Place Branding and Public Diplomacy*, 6(4), 316–332.

Palmer, C. (1999). Tourism and the symbols of identity. *Tourism Management*. 20(3), 313-321.

Palonen, E. (2013). Millennial politics of architecture: myths and nationhood in Budapest. *Nationalities Papers. The Journal of Nationalism and Ethnicity*, 41(4), 536-551.

Papp, Z. & Raffay, Á. (2011). Factors influencing the tourism competitiveness of former socialist countries. *Human Geographies*, 5(2), 21-30.

Park, S. Y. & Petrick, J. (2006). Destinations' Perspectives of Branding. *Annals of Tourism Research*, 33(1), 262-265.

Petrakos, G. (2012). Integration, spatial dynamics and regional policy dilemmas in the European Union. *Discussion Paper Series*, 18(2), 27-40.

Petrella, R. (1996). Globalization and internalization: the dynamics of the emerging world order. In R. Boyer, & D. Drache (Eds.) *States against Markets: the limits of globalization*, (pp. 62-83), London: Routledge.

Pine, J. & Gilmore, J. (1999) *The Experience Economy. Work is Theatre and Every Business a Stage*. USA: Harvard Business Press.

Povilanskas, R. & Armaitienė, A. (2010). Marketing Power of Actor-Networks – The Key to Tourism Competitiveness. In A. Clarke (Ed.) *Constructing Central Europe: Tourism Competitiveness*, (pp. 107-122), Veszprem: Pannonia University Press.

Prayag, G. & Ryan, C. (2012). Antecedents of Tourists' Loyalty to Mauritius: The role and influence of destination Image, place attachment, personal involvement, and Satisfaction. *Journal of Travel Research*, 51(3), 342-356.

Pride, R. (2002). Brand Wales: "Natural Revival". In N. Morgan, A. Pritchard and R. Pride (Eds.) *Destination Branding: Creating the unique destination proposition* (pp. 109-123), Oxford: Butterworth-Heinemann.

Pritchard, A. & Morgan, N.J. (2001). Culture, identity and tourism representation: marketing Cymru or Wales?. *Tourism Management*, 22(1), 167-179.

Rakić, T. & Chambers, D. (2012). Rethinking the consumption of places. *Annals of Tourism Research*, 39(3), 1612-1633.

Rainisto, S. (2003). *Success factors of place Marketing: A study of place marketing practices in Northern Europe and the United States*, Unpublished PhD thesis. Helsinki University of Technology.

Ren, C. & Ooi, C.S. (2013). Auto-communicating micro-Orientalism: articulating 'Denmark' in China at the Shanghai Expo. *Asia Europe Journal*, 11(2), 129-145.

Robson, C. (1993). *Real World Research, A Resource for Social Scientists and Practitioner-Researchers*. Oxford: Blackwell.

Rockower, P. (2012). Recipes for gastrodiplomacy. *Place Branding and Public Diplomacy*, 8(4), 235-246.

Sakellariou, E. & Karantinou, K. (2013). Global Front End of Product Innovation: A Guiding Framework for Multinational Organizations, 3rd *International Conference on Quantitative and Qualitative Research on Administration Sciences*, Athens, 23-24 May 2013.

Sartori, A., Mottironi, C. & Antonioli-Corigliano, M. (2012). Tourist Destination brand equity and internal stakeholders: An empirical research. *Journal of Vacation Marketing*, 18(4), 327-340.

Sauer, C. (1984). *The Morphology of Landscape*. California: University of California Publications in Geography.

Scott, N., Suwaree, A., Peivi Ding, A. & Xu, H. (2011). Tourism branding and nation building in China. *International Journal of Culture, Tourism and Hospitality Research*, 5(3), 227-234.

Siomkos, G. & Tsiamis, J. (2004). *Strategic Electronic Marketing*. Athens: Stamouli.

Shackley, M. (1998). *Visitor Management Case Studies for World Heritage Sites*. Oxford: Butterworth-Heinemann.

Skinner, H. (2008). The emergence and development of place marketing's confused identity. *Journal of Marketing Management*, 24(9/10), 915-928.

Skinner, H. & Kubacki, K. (2007). Unravelling the complex relationship between nationhood, national and cultural identity, and place branding. *Place Branding and Public Diplomacy*, 3 (4), 305–316.

Smith, A. D. (1984). National Identity and Myths of Ethnic Descent. *Research in Social Movements, Conflict and Change*, 7(1), 95-130.

Smith, A. D. (1991). *National Identity*. London: Penguin Books.

Smith, A. D. (1996). Culture, community and territory: the politics of ethnicity and nationalism. *International Affairs*, 72(3), 445-458.

Smith, M. (2004). Seeing a new side to seasides: culturally regenerating the English seaside town. *International Journal of Tourism Research*, 6(1), 17-28.

Smith, S. & Darlington, K. (2010). Emotional ecologies as brands: Towards a theory of occasioned local feeling. *Place Branding and Public Diplomacy*, 6(2), 112–123.

Souder, L. (2010). A Free-market Model for Media Ethics: Adam Smith's Looking Glass. *Journal of Mass Media Ethics*, 25(1), 53-64.

Stern, B., Zinkhan, G., & Holbrook, M. (2002). The Netvertising Image Communication Model (NICM) and Construct Definition. *Journal of Advertising*, 31(3), 15-27.

Statistics Office of Regione Veneto (2009). *Veneto: sharing facts-comparing facts. Statisitcal Report 2009*. Padova: University of Padova.

Stavrianea, K. (2010). *The Antecedents of Service Consumer Loyalty*. Athens: PhD Dissertation, University of Economics and Business.

Szondi, G. (2010). From image management to relationship building: A public relations approach to nation branding. *Place Branding and Public Diplomacy*, 6(4), 333-343.

Thompson, J. (1995). The Media and Modernity. *A Social Theory of the Media*. USA: Stanford University Press.

Thornton, P., Ribeiro-Soviano, D. & Urbano, D. (2011). Socio-cultural factors and entrepreneurial activity: An overview. *International Small Business Journal*, 29(2): 105-118.

Thlikidou-Stogianni, E. (2003). *Post-modern Marketing: review*. Thlikidou: University Studio Press (in Greek).

Tomaras, P. & Frigkas, G. (2008). Consumer ethnocentricism in Greece. Adaptation of the CETSscale questionnaire. *Business and Management*, 10.

Van den Abeele, A. (1990). Tourism and Heritage: Enemies or Allies? in Heritage and Tourism- ICOMOS European Conference, University of Kent- 27th-30th March 1990, 1-22, UK: ICOMOS.

Velissariou, E., Galagala, A. & Karathanos, A. (2009). Wine tourism. Planning and Development of a wine route network in the region of Thessaly in Greece. *Tourismos*, 4(4), 311-330.

Veloutsou, C. (2008). Branding: a constantly developing concept. *Journal of Brand Management*, 15(5), 299-300.

Vinieratou, M., Georgiou, A., Glytsi, E., Kioukas, A., Koskina, A., Bousoulega, X., Oikonomou, M. Skoura, B., Taxopoulou, I. & Champouri-Ioanninou, A. (2003). *Cultural Policy and Management*. Patra: Hellenic Open University.

Vlachvei, A., Notta, O. & Ananiadis, I. (2009). Does advertising matter? An application to the Greek wine industry. *British Food Journal*, 111(4), 686-698.

Weidenfeld, A., William, A., & Butler, R. (2010). Knowledge transfer and innovation among attractions, *Annals of Tourism Research*, 37(3), 604-626.

Whalley, A. (2010). *Strategic Marketing*. Whalley & Ventus Publishing ApS.

Yin, R. K. (1993). *Applications of Case Study Research*. California: Sage.

Ying, F. (2005). Branding the nation: What is being branded? *Journal of Vacation Marketing*, 12(1), 4-13.

Yuksel, A., Yuksel, F. & Bilim, Y. (2010). Destination attachment: Effects on customer satisfaction and cognitive, affective and conative loyalty. *Tourism Management*, 31(2), 274-284.

Zarantonello, L. & Schmitt, B.H. (2010) Using the Brand Experience Scale to Profile Consumers and Predict consumer Behaviour. *Journal of Brand Management*, 17(7), 532-540.

Zeppel, H. & Hall, M. C. (1991). Selling Art and History: Cultural Heritage and Tourism. *The Journal of Tourism Studies*, 2(1), 29-45.

Zotos, Y. (2008). *Advertising, Development, Effectiveness* (in Greek), Thessaloniki: University Studio Press.

AUTHOR CONTACT INFORMATION

Dr. Androniki Kavoura
Assistant Professor
Department of Marketing
Technological Educational Institute of Athens
Agios Spiridonos, 12210 Aigaleo, Greece
Telephone: +30 2109828455
E-mail: nkavoura@teiath.gr

INDEX

#

20th century, 25, 51
21st century, 51, 64

A

access, 22, 26, 35, 54, 68, 72
accessibility, 16, 54
accommodation, 16, 36, 69
advertsing, ix, x, 9, 10, 11, 13, 14, 16, 17,
    19, 23, 27, 28, 29, 32, 33, 34, 40, 41, 50,
    54, 58, 62, 64, 65, 66, 69, 70, 72, 75, 76
aesthetic, 36
affirming, 20
agencies, 4, 49, 62
agriculture, 19
ambassadors, 33
architects, 16
Asia, 58, 68, 74
aspiration, 30
assessment, 17
attachment, 38, 40, 52, 73, 76
attitudes, 13, 49, 53
attribution, 20
audits, 23
Austria, 20, 55, 70
authenticity, 17
authorities, 21, 38, 45, 54, 58, 62, 63
awareness, 5, 44

B

bank debts, 3
banks, 10
behavioral dimension, 36
behaviors, 2
benefits, 4, 20, 30, 43, 47, 49
blogs, 69
bonding, 40, 63
bonds, 38, 62
brand image, 30, 42, 51, 55
brand loyalty, 31, 67, 70
bureaucracy, 40
business model, 4
businesses, ix, 3, 4, 5, 6, 9, 10, 11, 13, 14,
    19, 35, 47, 49, 50, 51

C

campaigns, x, 13, 14, 27, 41
capitalism, 2
case studies, xi, 18
case study, 18, 55, 69
catalysis, 3
Central Europe, 73
certification, 20
challenges, 68
China, 74
Christianity, 22
circulation, 1
citizens, 4, 19, 57, 62

D

E

T

U

V

varieties, 44

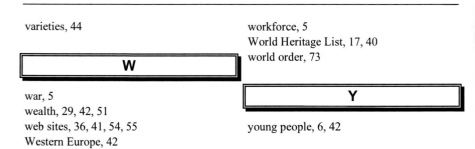

W

war, 5
wealth, 29, 42, 51
web sites, 36, 41, 54, 55
Western Europe, 42

workforce, 5
World Heritage List, 17, 40
world order, 73

Y

young people, 6, 42